The National Museum of Wales

A Companion Guide to the National Art Gallery

Mark Evans and Oliver Fairclough

The National Museum of Wales

A Companion Guide to the National Art Gallery

National Museum of Wales/Cardiff
in association with
Lund Humphries/London

First published in Great Britain in 1993 by
National Museum of Wales
Cathays Park
Cardiff CF1 3NP
in association with
Lund Humphries Publishers
Park House
1 Russell Gardens
London NW11 9NN

British Library Cataloguing-in-Publication Data
A catalogue record for this book is available from
the British Library

Lund Humphries ISBN 0 85331 642 2
National Museum of Wales ISBN 0 7200 0584 x

FRONTISPIECE
The façade of the National Museum of Wales

Designed by Alan Bartram
Typeset by August Filmsetting, St Helens
Printed and bound in Great Britain by
British Gas Wales

Contents

Sponsor's Preface

British Gas Wales welcomes the opportunity to sponsor this companion guide to the rich and varied art collections of the National Museum of Wales, published to mark the opening of its new art galleries by Her Majesty The Queen. Reading the introduction about the early history of the Museum, I was deeply impressed by the determination of its founders to establish an art collection of quality for the education and enjoyment of the people of Wales. At British Gas Wales we are similarly committed to this ideal of public service and I hope that this informative guide will make this distinguished collection more widely known.

JOHN HINCHLIFFE
Regional Chairman, British Gas Wales

Foreword

The generous offer of British Gas Wales to sponsor this guide to our newly re-displayed art collections presents the welcome opportunity to review a century of endeavour. In 1907 the founding fathers of the National Museum envisaged a collection which would set the fine and applied arts of Wales in an international context. Their vision became a reality within the brief span of a single lifetime, largely through the generosity of such collectors as Gwendoline and Margaret Davies, W. S. de Winton, James Pyke Thompson, Sir William Goscombe John, E. Morton Nance and, most recently, Derek Williams and Sir Leslie Joseph. At Cardiff one can study the two-century-old dialogue between painters and the Welsh landscape beside masterpieces of the Classical tradition and the spectacular achievements of the Impressionists and Post-Impressionists. The 'New Sculpture' movement may be compared with an impressive group of contemporary French bronzes. Similarly, the supreme achievement of the applied arts in Wales – the porcelains of Swansea and Nantgarw – can be viewed in detail beside magnificent displays of British and continental ceramics of similar date. I hope that the scope of our collections – spanning the Renaissance to the present day, ranging from oil paintings to japanware, by artists little known outside Wales as well as international celebrities – will encourage creative leaps of the imagination which are frequently inhibited by larger and more specialised collections.

Since 1987, with special assistance from the Welsh Office and the generous help of several foundations and donors, our art galleries have been doubled in size and air-conditioned to the highest possible international standard; the collections have been comprehensively and methodically re-displayed and new conservation studios, stores and other facilities provided. This has entailed a great deal of sustained hard work by museum staff and outside contractors. I am profoundly grateful for all their efforts, but would like to express my special appreciation of the contribution of the Keeper of Art and his staff. It is in large measure through their efforts that a National Gallery of Wales has been created within the National Museum of Wales, providing a fitting home for our superb art collections. This has been commemorated by the present illustrated guide, generously sponsored by British Gas Wales. I hope that it will encourage old friends to return and will introduce a great art gallery to a new public, both at home and abroad.

ALISTAIR WILSON
Director
National Museum of Wales

Acknowledgements

The publication of this guide marks the rebuilding, extension and redisplay of the art galleries at the National Museum of Wales, begun in 1987 and completed in 1993. During this period we have incurred numerous obligations. I would like to place on record the gratitude of the Department of Art to everyone concerned with the project, especially its architect, John Phillips of Alex Gordon and Partners, and our Buildings Officer, Basil Thomas. With extraordinary energy, patience and good humour they have transformed our hopes and plans into reality. The achievements of the last six years would have been impossible without the total commitment of all members of the Department of Art. The practical arrangements of preparation and display have been handled with exemplary care by Kate Lowry, Jim France, Judi Pinkham, Mike Jones and Keith Bowen. Mark Evans and Oliver Fairclough have planned the displays, written the labels and the text of this guide. I am also grateful to Jon Astbury, Katy Barron, Lisa Childs, Gemma Curtin, Peter David, Rachel Duberley, Tim Egan, Rosa Freeman, Avril Haynes, Sarah Herring, Mary Kilpatrick, Christine Mackay, Rachel Oliver, Paul Rees and Sylvia Richards. Elsewhere in the National Museum considerable assistance has been provided by Louise Carey, Cliff Darch, Bryn Davies, Tony Hadland, John Kenyon, Colin Plain, Hywel Rees, John Rowlands, Kevin Thomas and Jim Wild. If the past donors and curators who built this collection could see its new home I believe they would consider themselves well served by posterity.

TIMOTHY STEVENS
Keeper of Art

Introduction:
The Growth of a Collection

1. William Menelaus (1818-82)

By the middle of the nineteenth century there were about sixty museums in Britain, mostly administered by universities or learned societies. The greatest institutions – the British Museum and the National Gallery – were themselves based upon private collections and founded by Acts of Parliament in 1753 and 1824. Municipal authorities, enabled by the Museums Act of 1845 to fund museums and inspired by the success of the 1851 Great Exhibition, began to establish comparable institutions: the Liverpool Museum in 1851, Glasgow Art Gallery and Museum in 1854 and Birmingham Museum and Art Gallery in 1867. In 1862 Cardiff was the first Welsh authority to utilise the Public Libraries Act of 1855 when it founded a Free Library and Museum with an annual corporation grant of £450.

Donations trickled in but the new institution received no works of art until 1870, the year of the Cardiff *Fine Art and Industrial Exhibition*. One of many shows held in emulation of the Great Exhibition, this display of art, antiquities, industrial machinery and curiosities occupied an area of about 900 sq m in the Drill Hall. The sculptor James Milo Griffith (1843-97) submitted several sculptures, five of which he gave to the museum. Both the 1870 exhibition and its successor held in 1881 were intended to raise funds for the construction and fitting out of a new Free Library and Museum building in Trinity Street. These premises opened in 1882, in time to receive their first substantial fine-art collection. This was the bequest of thirty-six paintings, including Tissot's *Bad news (The parting)*, assembled by William Menelaus (1818-82), Managing Partner of the steelworks at Dowlais. The same year the museum spent £20 on a group of Swansea and Nantgarw porcelain. This was chosen by the chemist and scientist Robert Drane (1834-1914), under whose guidance a collection of Welsh ceramics was built up during the 1880s and 1890s. At the same time the Unitarian corn merchant James Pyke Thompson (1846-97) was assembling his own collection, mainly of nineteenth-century watercolours. In 1888 he placed part of this on public display in a small gallery named Turner House adjoining his home in Penarth, a few miles from Cardiff. Following his election as chairman of its Fine-Arts Sub-Committee in 1895, Pyke Thompson lent Cardiff Museum and Art Gallery another substantial part of his collection. In 1898 he bequeathed 149 watercolours, including Turner's *Ewenny Priory*, a small number of oil paintings, a portfolio of etchings and three cases of British and continental porcelain, together with £6000 towards the cost of building a new art gallery. Pyke Thompson's collection was reunited in 1921 when the trustees of Turner House presented the building and its contents to the National Museum of Wales.

During the nineteenth century it was increasingly perceived that actual or would-be nation states required such institutions as universities, libraries and museums both for educational reasons and as a badge of nationhood. A classic instance of the link between museums and nationalism is provided by the Hungarian National Museum, founded as early as 1802, from whose steps the lyric poet Alexander Petoefi launched the 1848 uprising against Hapsburg rule. At Edinburgh the National Gallery of Scotland was set up in 1850 and the Royal Museum of Scotland in 1854. In Dublin the foundation of the National Gallery of Ireland in 1854 was similarly followed by that of the National Museum of Ireland in 1877. Lacking the focal point of a capital city, Welsh national consciousness awoke more slowly. The university colleges became the federal University of Wales in 1893 and the need for a National Museum and Library

2. James Pyke Thompson (1846-97)

was a theme of the 1893 Pontypridd Eisteddfod. The need was also regularly brought up in the House of Commons until 1905 when the government set up a committee of the Privy Council to decide where such an institution could be based. In tune with these aspirations the committee of Cardiff Museum and Art Gallery had already begun to draw up plans for a new building in Cathays Park. In 1901 it resolved on a change of name to the Welsh Museum of Natural History, Arts and Antiquities 'to bring the title of the institution into line with the growing national character of its collections'. The offer of the extant building and collections, a four-acre site in Cathays Park, Pyke Thompson's bequest and an additional cash deposit towards new premises were sufficient to secure the National Museum for Cardiff, rather than Swansea or Caernarvon. Following the grant of a royal foundation charter in 1907, work on the new building began in 1912 according to the designs of A. Dunbar Smith and Cecil C. Brewer. Towards the end of 1922 the art collections were transferred from Trinity Street to the National Museum of Wales, which was officially opened in 1927 following the completion of its main hall and some galleries.

In 1895 Pyke Thompson had drawn up a report on the future development of the fine-art collections at the Cardiff Museum and Art Gallery which advocated a dual strategy. It was acknowledged that 'Local artists, and Welsh artists whether living or deceased, should be represented more or less fully, according to their position in the world of art', and that 'Local subjects, again, we should lay ourselves open to acquire, whenever the execution comes up to a certain standard of excellence'. He continued: 'But beyond this, our choice should be limited to the very first painters of the day, unless under very exceptional circumstances.' In 1906 his friend and executor Sir Frederick Wedmore (1844-1921), art critic of the London *Standard* and Art Advisor to the Welsh Museum, observed, 'it is clearly our business to represent as far as possible the best Welsh work, provided always that it attains to a standard of excellence'. He recommended the acquisition of 'a really fine Richard Wilson' while, 'Other Welsh artists, not excluding living ones, should ... be bought at reasonable prices, as opportunity offers'. Wedmore added, 'as we exist, it is admitted, not only to show what good Art Wales may have produced, but also to represent Art generally – whether English, or even Foreign ... to see that the modern phases of Art are not forgotten'. The 1907 and 1911 foundation charters of the National Museum echoed the need for a twin-track policy. These stated that while its objectives should be 'mainly and primarily the complete illustration of the ... art history ... of Wales', the museum should also 'further the collection preservation and maintenance of all objects and things (including pictures engravings statuary and all works of fine art of any kind) whether connected or not with Wales' to further the aims of Welsh educational institutions in particular and literary and scientific research in general. In 1913 the Welsh sculptor and founder-member of the museum's Court of Governors, Sir William Goscombe John, also argued that it should: 'Concentrate upon the purchase of works by artists connected with Wales ... and buy occasionally, for the purposes of comparison and study, works of art of various kinds by distinguished modern artists of other nations, both British and foreign.'

To help rectify the lack of modern works in the collection, in 1907 Wedmore was empowered to utilise the interest from Pyke Thompson's bequest towards the building of a new art gallery to purchase pictures. The Museum Committee

3. Sir Frederick Wedmore (1844-1921)

4. Sir William Goscombe John (1860-1952)
oil painting by George Roilos (*fl.*1900-10),
NMW A 588

ventured to hope that 'any works purchased out of it, though necessarily small, will be of real artistic merit; and ... will eventually lead to the formation of a definite picture fund worthy of Cardiff'. Given the inadequacy of this sum, Wedmore made a series of remarkably effective acquisitions between 1907 and 1920. These included oils by the recent or contemporary French painters Courbet, Bonvin, Ribot, Boudin, Isabey, Lépine and Le Sidaner and several of the more progressive British artists of the day. These included Philip Wilson Steer's *The schoolgirl* and representative works by William Nicholson, James Pryde, Philip Connard, John Lavery and Laura Knight. In 1914 the National Museum, encouraged by this success, made its own first major purchase, spending £450 on George Clausen's *In the fields in June* on the suggestion of Goscombe John. Unfortunately when Wedmore advocated the purchase of Sickert's *Eglise Saint Jacques, Dieppe* for £90 in 1918, it was vehemently opposed by the conservatively minded Keeper of Art, Isaac Williams (1875-1939): 'It is an example of the extreme impressionist school which Sir Frederick seems to admire so much. In my opinion this particular class of work is quite unsuitable for an important public collection as it only seems to excite the eccentric imagination of a very small number of people who mistake their unhappy affliction for genuine artistic perception.'

In 1902 the Cardiff Museum Committee had decided that 'the collections of Welsh porcelains and earthenwares required for their educational development a representative series of British ceramic products generally', and with a government grant from the Board of Education began to assemble a collection of seventeenth- and eighteenth-century English pottery. In 1904 this was complemented by a loan of Chelsea and Bow porcelain from the banker W. S. de Winton (1856-1929). De Winton subsequently made a number of gifts and in 1912 he offered to lend the National Museum 150 pieces of eighteenth-century continental porcelain. By 1916 the loan, which also included many English pieces, had grown to over two thousand objects, a year later it became a gift and de Winton continued to add to it up to his death in 1929. The de Winton collection transformed the character and content of the ceramics collection. Its great strength is its documentary importance as it consists largely of marked pieces. Bernard Rackham (1876-1964), Keeper of Ceramics at the Victoria and Albert Museum, wrote in 1919:

the National Museum now possesses ... the best public collection in this Kingdom of Continental porcelain, other than figures ... the sections of German porcelain, especially early Meissen ... and Anspach, Ludwigsburg and the Dutch section, are particularly strong ... I doubt whether any Museum in Holland has a better. It is no exaggeration to say that students of Continental porcelain must now make a pilgrimage to Cardiff ... The Welsh Museum is to be congratulated on having a collection worthy of a national collection.

In 1913-14 the National Museum mounted two major art exhibitions in its temporary gallery at Cardiff City Hall which embodied the policy of presenting both 'Welsh artists, whether living or deceased' and 'the very first painters of the day'. The *Exhibition of Works by certain Modern Artists of Welsh Birth or Extraction* was actually the second of these, being mounted between 5 December 1913 and 28 February 1914, but its planning had begun earlier. Its terms of reference probably suggested by T. Mardy Rees's book, *Welsh Painters, Engravers, Sculptors*

5. Wilfred de Winton (1856-1929)

(*1527-1911*), published at Caernarfon in 1912, this exhibition included eighty-one works by thirty-six artists. Its core consisted of works by Goscombe John, Frank Brangwyn and Christopher Williams supplemented. on the strength of their Welsh forebears, by G. F. Watts, Arthur Hughes and Sir Edward Burne-Jones. Much the most progressive painter included was Augustus John, whose patron Lord Howard de Walden contributed £100 towards the expenses of the show. The anonymously titled *Loan Exhibition of Paintings* held between 4 February and 28 March 1913 had a short gestation period, arising from a suggestion made by the painter Murray Urquhart (1880-1972) the previous December. With the exception of a dozen or so works borrowed from Wedmore and other sources, this was actually the début of the extraordinary collection of Gwendoline Davies (1882-1951) and Margaret Davies (1884-1963), the granddaughters of David Davies of Llandinam (1818-90), a self-made man who had made a fortune from contracting. The sisters not only agreed to lend their pictures, but also with characteristic generosity undertook to pay for the exhibition. This included sixty-one works by twenty-seven artists, including Constable, Raeburn, Romney, Turner and Wilson. Its nucleus comprised major groups of paintings by Corot, Daumier, Millet, Whistler and Monet, two sculptures by Rodin and a range of landscapes and genre scenes by continental artists of the later nineteenth century. Such a display of French art had seldom before been seen in Britain, causing Hugh Blaker (1873-1936), the curator of the Holburne of Menstrie Museum in Bath and an advisor of the Davies sisters, to exclaim, 'It is hardly necessary to state that the exhibition is the greatest artistic event in the history of Wales'. Although local papers gave the exhibition far less favourable reviews than the national press, it was well attended, receiving 26,073 visitors, including 3489 school children; a daily average of over 500 people. Although also judged 'a great attraction and ... much appreciated', the *Exhibition of Works by certain Modern Artists of Welsh Birth or Extraction* proved less successful. The following winter it was viewed by 15,328 visitors, only 427 of whom were schoolchildren; an average of fewer than 200 people per day.

The Davies sisters had begun to collect in 1908, initially favouring works by revered British painters of the previous century as well as Corot, Millet and other well-established French artists. Blaker encouraged them to develop an interest in Daumier, Manet and Rodin. In 1912-13 they broke new ground, acquiring an early Manet, Renoir's *The Parisienne*, four Rodin bronzes and two marbles and seven late Monets. The sisters continued to purchase enthusiastically through the First World War, assembling notable collections of Daumier, Carrière and Augustus John and additional works by Manet, Renoir, Monet and Rodin. Their collection was effectively completed in 1918-20 with the addition of three Cézanne oils and two drawings, representative groups by Pissarro and Vlaminck and van Gogh's spectacular *Rain at Auvers*. It is unclear when Gwendoline and Margaret Davies first entertained the notion of leaving their collection to the National Museum of Wales, but they lent it Rodin's *The kiss* and *Illusions fallen to earth* following the close of their exhibition in 1913. By the following year they and their brother David were already deeply involved with the institution's affairs, jointly giving the museum building account a sum of £5000, rather more than the treasury grant of £4800 and almost half its total receipts for the year. The sisters gave a further £5000 in 1916, in which year the treasury grant towards capital expenditure was £18,800 and the total of other donations towards the

6. Gwendoline Davies (1882-1951)

7. Margaret Davies (1884-1963)

building fund slightly under £3500. In 1919 Gwendoline Davies, mindful of the museum's financial difficulties, offered help through the National Art-Collections Fund towards the purchase of the cartoon for Augustus John's monumental *Canadian war memorial*. Even with assistance, its purchase price of £2500 remained well beyond the institution's means. In 1925, two years before the official opening of the new museum building, the sisters augmented its art displays with the additional long-term loan of nine Augustus John oils and a Brangwyn. These pictures, the Rodins lent in 1913, two further works by the sculptor and a Burne-Jones were made an outright gift in 1940, becoming the first works from the Davies collection to enter the museum.

In 1913, guided by Goscombe John's note on *The Method of purchasing Works of Art* and a draft list of artists of Welsh birth or extraction prepared by his friend the painter T. H. Thomas (1839-1915), the National Museum made a spectacular addition to its collection of Welsh paintings by purchasing Richard Wilson's *Caernarvon Castle* for £380. During the First World War the institution's purchase grant was slashed, to less than £300 in 1917. Despite a partial recovery, this seldom exceeded £2000 per annum during the inter-war years plummeted to under £1000 during the Second World War and did not regain its 1915 peak of £2393 until 1951. In 1919-20 the total grant for specimens and books was only £1114, moving the then Keeper of Art to complain to his committee of 'the utter impossibility of attempting to build up a Welsh National Art Collection worthy of the name on the ridiculously small sums of money which appear to be available for this purpose.' Under these circumstances the museum had no option but to concentrate on acquiring eighteenth- and nineteenth-century prints, drawings and minor oil paintings of Welsh subjects at modest prices, punctuated by individual more ambitious purchases, including: Richard Wilson oils at £273 in 1925, £300 in 1936 and £525 in 1937; a John Gibson marble at £175 in 1928; and a monumental Penry Williams at £40 in 1933. When two large but unfinished pictures by Burne-Jones appeared at Lord Leverhulme's sale in 1926, Sir William Goscombe John purchased them for the museum and was reimbursed £86 16s by a grateful but impecunious council. By comparison, through the inter-war years gifts remained a more important source of acquisitions. Richard Wilson's *View of Dover* was given by subscribers in 1928 and the National Art-Collections Fund bore most of the costs of his *Pembroke town and castle* in 1930. Goscombe John was much the most regular donor, giving hundreds of sculptures, prints, paintings and drawings in a series of almost annual gifts between 1911 and 1948. In addition to much of his own work, this included a distinguished group of statues by his colleagues in the New Sculpture movement and bronzes by Carpeaux and Rodin. His finest gift was Alfred Gilbert's spectacular bronze *Icarus*, presented in 1938. Between 1929 and 1935 the painter Frank Brangwyn also made generous gifts of his own work, including the monumental cartoons *A heavy gun in action* and *A tank in action*. Another important benefactor of the inter-war period was the Cardiff collector F. E. Andrews (1858-1943), whose gifts included several major pieces of Welsh ceramics and a fine collection of medieval and later ivories.

The museum's first Assistant Keeper of Art, David Baxandall (1905-92), was appointed in 1928. He later recalled: 'I was very young and an enthusiastic champion of David Jones, Ben Nicholson, and a few other 7 & 5 types, but I knew of no one in Wales who, *if* they knew their work, did not think it nonsense.'

8. Ernest Morton Nance (1868-1952)

When in 1932 the museum's Art and Archaeology committee was offered a gift of contemporary drawings, including two works by David Jones, 'tempers grew warm'. Baxandall 'pleaded and argued for what seemed a terribly long time … and eventually there was a singularly grudging acceptance.' In 1935 public consciousness of modern art began to improve with the foundation of what was to become the Contemporary Art Society for Wales, which mounted the *Contemporary Welsh Art Exhibition*, at Aberystwyth, Swansea and the National Museum. This exhibition of 202 works was dominated by J. D. Innes, Cedric Morris, David Jones, Gwen John and, above all, Augustus John. From it the museum purchased a Gwen John oil for £20 and prints by Blair Hughes-Stanton and David Jones. The same year, the National Art-Collections Fund presented J. D. Innes's *Canigou in snow*. In 1936 the Contemporary Art Society gave the National Museum the first Augustus John drawing to enter its permanent collection, followed by a Winifred Nicholson and a drawing by Henri Gaudier-Brzeska in 1938 and Augustus John's celebrated portrait of *Dylan Thomas* in 1942. A friend of Baxandall was Jim Ede (1895-1990), the Cardiff-born curator and authority on contemporary art, best known for rehabilitating Gaudier-Brzeska's reputation and founding the Kettle's Yard Gallery in Cambridge. In 1940, a year after his promotion to Keeper of Art and shortly before joining the RAF for the duration of the war, Baxandall mounted an exhibition from Ede's collection of Gaudier-Brzeska sculptures and drawings. During the Second World War the museum's primary art collections were in secure storage, but a series of mainly contemporary art exhibitions was mounted in the Cathays Park building with the assistance of such bodies as the Contemporary Art Society, the Contemporary Art Society for Wales and the Council for the Encouragement of Music and the Arts.

Shortly after the end of the war Batoni's *Williams Wynn* group portrait was bought for £230 from the Wynnstay sale and the museum was presented by the National Art-Collections Fund with Mengs' portrait of *Richard Wilson* from the same collection. As the purchase grant was still pegged on or below its pre-war level, gifts such as the 1947 Nettlefold bequest of bronzes and the Taylor and Clark donations of British porcelain remained a more important source of acquisitions. In 1952 the museum's holdings of Welsh ceramics were more than doubled by the Morton Nance bequest. Born in Cardiff, Ernest Morton Nance (1868-1952) was the author of the monumental *Pottery and Porcelain of Swansea and Nantgarw*, published in 1942. His bequest, which included many rare and provenanced pieces, confirmed the museum's longstanding role as the principal public collection of Welsh pottery and porcelain.

Also in 1952, Gwendoline Davies's collection of 109 paintings, drawings and sculpture was bequeathed to the museum, whose *Annual Report* observed: 'By this princely benefaction the character of the Department of Art has been transformed, so that it now takes a high place among the major art-collections of Great Britain.' Rising to this challenge, in 1957 assistance from the National Art-Collections Fund, local industry and private subscribers was marshalled to raise £6450, more than three times the usual annual purchase grant, to acquire Canaletto's *Bacino di San Marco*. During the 1950s the museum began to acquire major pieces of Welsh-provenanced silver to complement the large loan collection deposited in 1922 by the Monmouth-born Sir Charles Jackson (1840-1923), author of what remains the standard work on British hallmarks. Purchases

1. Art in Wales from the Middle Ages to the Enlightenment

10

Medieval Wales was a notoriously poor and politically chaotic region, divided from the eleventh century among native princes, Norman marcher lords and the growing royal domain of the King of England. Towns were few and small, while bishoprics were poor and extended over large areas. After the death in battle of the last native Welsh prince, Llywelyn ap Gruffydd, in 1282, the Plantaganets extended and consolidated their authority. In 1400 Owain Glyn Dwr assumed the title of Prince of Wales and briefly overran almost the whole of the principality. After his defeat Henry V enacted severe laws to discourage further rebellion. Nevertheless in 1485 Henry Tudor began his successful campaign against Richard III with a recruiting march from Milford Haven to Shrewsbury. The legal and administrative structure of Wales was finally brought into line with that of England under Henry VIII by the Acts of Union of 1536 and 1543.

In Wales only Tintern and St David's can compare with the magnificent abbeys and cathedrals of the English borders, such as Gloucester, Tewkesbury, Hereford, Worcester and Chester. By contrast the ring of castles with which Edward I encircled

North Wales from Flint to Harlech are the most spectacular fortifications of thirteenth-century Europe. During the late Middle Ages discriminating patrons throughout Northern Europe acquired paintings, tapestries and illuminated manuscripts from the leading workshops in the Flemish cities of Ghent and Bruges. One of the most distinguished British commissions of the fifteenth century was Hans Memling's triptych purchased by Sir John Donne of Kidwelly around 1480 and now in the National Gallery in London. Donne's brother-in-law, William Lord Hastings, was a close friend of Edward IV, Chamberlain of North Wales and Constable of Harlech Castle. His magnificent Flemish book of hours, now in the British Library, includes a rare full-page miniature of *St David*. Henry VII and Henry VIII increasingly turned to Italian masters but the Low Countries remained a major source of artists and works of art for British patrons throughout the Renaissance. Outstanding Welsh commissions of the mid-sixteenth century include the silver ewer and basin from Bruges with the arms of the Mostyn family of Flintshire and the portrait of *Katheryn of Berain*, probably painted by the Friesian artist Adriaen van Cronenburgh.

The Tudors were mindful of their ancestry, incorporating the red dragon as one of the supporter figures of the arms of England. Their accession encouraged a flight of Welsh gentry to London. A typical, if spectacular, case is that of the Cecils of Allt-yr-ynys. In 1507 David Cecil became a Yeoman of the Chamber to Henry VII. His grandson William Cecil, Baron Burghley, was Elizabeth I's chief minister. Lord Burghley had business interests in Wales and was proud of his family history, but he built the spectacular residences of Burghley House and Theobalds Park on his English estates. Although James I encouraged the wearing of leeks by Welshmen on St David's Day as a 'good and commendable fashion', his accession in 1603 marked the end of an era of Welsh influence at court.

Secular architecture and tomb sculpture flourished in Britain during the two centuries after the Reformation, but large-scale painting languished. The rudimentary epitaph-panels with members of the Stradling family, made in 1590 for their chapel in St Donat's Church, Llantwit Major are characteristic provincial examples of late Elizabethan memorial painting. Portraiture remained in demand in Protestant Britain and one cannot deny the charm of such late sixteenth- and early seventeenth-century portraits as *Henry Herbert 2nd Earl of Pembroke* and *Sir Thomas Mansel and his wife Jane*. However such works are barely comparable with continental paintings of similar date. The major British contribution to Renaissance painting lay in the field of the portrait miniature. Introduced in 1528-43 by the Flemish illuminator Lucas Horenbout and the German Hans Holbein, this art form flourished during the reigns of Elizabeth I and James I through the achievements of their court artists Nicholas Hilliard and Isaac Oliver.

Despite his political ineptitude Charles I was the greatest royal patron of the arts in British history. The king commissioned from Sir Peter Paul Rubens the monumental *Apotheosis of James I* for the ceiling of Inigo Jones's recently built Banqueting House, Whitehall. In 1632 Cornelius Johnson, of Flemish extraction and probably trained in Holland, was engaged as 'King's Painter'. The same year Rubens's great pupil Anthony Van Dyck was sworn in as his 'Principal Painter in Ordinary'. Charles's court sculptor was the Frenchman Hubert Le Sueur, who had previously served Louis XIII. His arrival in London in 1625 may be connected with the embassy of the Welsh courtier Lord Herbert of Cherbury to Paris in 1622-4. Lord Herbert was one of the most colourful personalities of the early Stuart court and a distinguished patron, commissioning one of the largest and most spectacular of Isaac Oliver's miniatures in 1610-14, as well as a bronze bust by Hubert Le Sueur in 1631.

The court was of central significance to seventeenth-century British art and the Civil War and Protectorate seriously dislocated patterns of patronage. After the Restoration there was a 'building boom' both in the fire-ravaged City of London and in the regions. The most spectacular Baroque mansions in Wales are Tredegar House near Newport, built for Sir William Morgan in 1664-72, and Powis Castle, totally remodelled for William, third Lord Powis, from 1665. During the later seventeenth century there was little that could usefully be described as a native 'British' school of painting. As before, the most distinguished painters came from abroad. Sir Peter Lely, who became 'Principal Painter' to Charles II in 1661, had been born in Westphalia and apprenticed in Haarlem. His successor, Sir Godfrey Kneller, came from Lübeck and studied in Holland and Italy before arriving in England in 1676. The two other leading portraitists of the late seventeenth and early eighteenth centuries were John Closterman, from Osnabrück who trained in Paris, and the Swede Michael Dahl who travelled to Paris, Venice and Rome before establishing himself in London in 1689. Charles II silver also draws heavily on Dutch prototypes. Baroque history and decorative painting in Britain was similarly dominated by the immigrant artists Antonio Verrio and Louis Laguerre, until their assistant Sir James Thornhill established his reputation during the first decade of the eighteenth century. Like their English contemporaries and relations, gentlemen from South and North Wales turned to these foreign painters resident in London when they required fashionable portraits. Examples include Sir John Aubrey of Llantrithyd, near Cowbridge, and Sir Roger Mostyn of Mostyn Hall, Flintshire, whose portraits by Closterman and Kneller are both in the National Museum.

In the late seventeenth century industrial enterprises proliferated on landed estates throughout Wales and after 1700 the mining of coal, iron, lead and copper brought a new wealth and confidence to parts of Monmouthshire, Glamorgan, Carmarthenshire, Cardiganshire and Flint. This encouraged much of the gentry, committed to trade, peace and low taxes, in Tory

11. Adriaen van Cronenburgh
(1520/3-1604)
Katheryn of Berain 1568
oil on panel
97.2 × 68.6 cm
Katheryn of Berain (1534/5-91) was the daughter of Tudur ap Robert Vychan of Berain, Denbighshire. She married four times and through her numerous children and step-children became known as the Mother of Wales. In 1567 she married Sir Richard Clough, a wealthy merchant from Denbigh, who lived in Antwerp and Hamburg. It is likely this portrait was painted in the northern Netherlands by the Friesian artist van Cronenburgh. The skull is symbolic of mortality.
Given by the Friends of the National Museum of Wales 1957.
NMW A 19

14

13

13. Isaac Oliver (*c*.1565-1617)
Henry, Prince of Wales
gum arabic on vellum stuck to card
6.6 × 5.3 cm
Born at Rouen, Oliver was brought
to London as a child. A leading
Court miniaturist from 1604, he
was a member of the household of
the Prince of Wales. Prince Henry
(1594-1612), the eldest son of
James I, died of typhoid. Unusually this portrait miniature retains
its original turned ivory case and
lid.
Purchased 1975. NMW A 718

14. British School (*c*.1625)
Sir Thomas Mansel and his wife Jane
oil on canvas
118 × 126 cm
The Mansels of Margam were one
of the wealthiest families in South
Wales. Thomas Mansel
(1556-1631) was MP for Glamorgan. Often at the court of James I,
he bought a baronetcy in 1611.
Husband and wife are touchingly
shown holding hands in this painting of about 1625. The marigold
held by Lady Mansel is perhaps a
symbol for their daughter, Mary.
Purchased 1984. NMW A 16

15

16

17

15. Hubert le Sueur (1610-58)
Edward Herbert, 1st Baron Herbert of Cherbury 1631
bronze
H 52 cm
Born at Montgomery Castle, Lord Herbert (1581/3-1648) lived there and at his Shropshire Manor of Cherbury. A celebrated philosopher, historian, swordsman, musician and equestrian, he was ambassador to France in 1619 and 1622-4. Le Sueur was born in France and probably learned the elements of Florentine Mannerist sculpture from Italians working in Paris.
Purchased jointly with the National Trust 1990. NMW A 271

16. (i) Cup, London 1580
silver with traces of gilding
maker's mark: SB a mullet above
H 28 cm
This Elizabethan drinking cup was given to St Mary's Church, Monmouth sometime after 1660 for use as a communion cup.
Lent by the Vicar and Parochial Church Council of Monmouth.
NMW A (L) 424

16. (ii) Standing bowl, London 1570
silver, parcel gilt
maker's mark: SL
DIAM 15.7 cm
Shallow bowls of this type were made *c.*1530-90 and were mainly used as drinking vessels. The inscription records that this one was given to the Anglesey parish of

Penmynydd by its squire, Con-
ingsby Williams, in 1707.
Lent by Rector and Parochial
Church Council of Llan-
fairpwllgwyngyll. NMW A (L) 478

17. Ewer and dish, London 169:
and 1693
silver gilt
maker's mark: RC in a dotted
circle
H (ewer) 24.6 cm, DIAM (dish)
63.5 cm
These are engraved with the arms
of Sir John Trevor (1638-1717) of
Brynkinalt, Denbighshire and his
wife Jane Mostyn. A cousin of the
infamous Judge Jeffreys, Trevor
was Speaker of the House of Commons between 1685 and 1695. At
first virulently anti-Catholic, then
a supporter of James II and finally
a Tory manager for William III,
he was disgraced for accepting
bribes.
Purchased 1945. NMW A 50,305
and 50,306

18. Cornelius Johnson
(1593-1661)
Sir Thomas Hanmer 1631
oil on canvas
77.5 × 62.2 cm
Sir Thomas Hanmer (1612-78) of
Hanmer, Flintshire was a page at
the court of Charles I. He was a
noted horticulturist, introducing
many new plants to his garden at
Bettisfield Park, Flintshire. Cornelius Johnson trained abroad
before setting up as a portraitist in
London. The restrained silvery
tonality of the portrait comple-
ments the refined, sensitive character of the sitter.
Purchased 1944. NMW A 40

**19. Pair of sconces, John
Bodington, London** 1710
Britannia-standard silver
H 31.8 cm
These wall-lights bear the arms of
William Herbert, 2nd Marquess of
Powis (c.1665-1745). They are
crowned with a ducal coronet, as
his Jacobite father had also been
created Duke of Powis by the
exiled James II, and were probably
made for his London house as he
did not regain Powis Castle and his
family's Montgomeryshire estates
until 1722.
Purchased 1959. NMW A 50,354
and 50,355

18

19

20. (i) Punch bowl, Richard Bayley, London 1743
silver
DIAM 24.4 cm
Inscribed in Latin to Master Parry and the men of Flint, and in a later hand 'Darren-Fawr'. This was a silver mine near Aberystwyth, reopened by Parry with miners from Flintshire. There was a major strike of silver there in 1742.
Purchased 1980. NMW A 50,494

20. (ii) Jug, John Smith II, London c.1700
silver
H 30.5 cm
Engraved 'The Mines of Bwlch-yr Esker-hir', and probably made of bullion from the lead and silver mine opened at Esgair-hir, Cardiganshire in 1690. It bears the arms of William Powell of Nanteos, one the shareholders.
Purchased 1958. NMW A 50,352

20

21

22

21. (i) Wine glass *c.*1750
wheel-engraved lead glass
H 16.2 cm
Engraved with the emblem of the Society of Sea-Sergeants, a social club with Jacobite sympathies formed by the gentry of the maritime counties of South Wales. Its last recorded meeting was at Haverfordwest in 1762.
Purchased 1975. NMW A 50,508

21. (ii) Wine glass *c.*1740
wheel-engraved lead glass
H 17.5 cm
One of a small group of glasses bearing the name or arms of Sir Watkin Williams Wynn of Wynnstay (1692-1749). From 1720 he was patron of the Cycle, a Jacobite dining club for which these glasses may have been made.
Given by the Friends of the National Museum of Wales 1975.
NMW A 50,507

22. Pair of candlesticks, **Lewis Pantin, London** 1734
silver
H 27 cm
These candlesticks are among the earliest English examples of full-blown Rococo silver. They were made for Sir Watkin Williams Wynn of Wynnstay, Denbighshire, the greatest land-owner in North Wales. A Jacobite sympathiser, he was a leader of the 'country party' in the House of Commons.
Purchased 1985. NMW A 50,498 and 50,499

23. Tureen, Chinese 1745-50
hard-paste porcelain
H 21.6 cm
The Stepneys of Llanelli, Carmarthenshire, were among several Welsh gentry families to commission Chinese porcelain services painted with their arms during the first half of the 18th century. The tureen is a European Baroque shape and the flowers which form part of the decoration are also Western in inspiration.
Purchased 1993. NMW A 31,110 and 31,111

24. Tray, Pontypool *c.*1765
japanned iron
38.8 × 52.5 cm
This was probably commissioned by the Hanbury family who owned the Pontypool ironworks, as it is painted with Kelmarsh Hall, Northamptonshire, the seat of their kinsman Thomas Hanbury, who died in 1722. The view and the inscription are taken from an engraving in John Bridges' *History of Northamptonshire*. Although this was not published until 1791, the illustrations were prepared shortly before the author's death in 1724.
Purchased 1960. NMW A 50,239

23

24

2. Old Masters from the Renaissance to the Enlightenment

The notion of the 'Old Master', an artist of distinguished skill universally acknowledged as a model of excellence, was current from the Renaissance until the Romantic period. It conforms to the view of the sixteenth-century art historian Giorgio Vasari that a rebirth of painting occurred in Trecento and Quattrocento Italy which culminated in the perfection of a 'correct' style during the lifetimes of Raphael and Michelangelo. These masters were originally 'modern' in distinction from the equally revered painters and sculptors of Classical Antiquity. They became 'old' when viewed in retrospect across a gulf of one or more centuries by theorists such as Sir Joshua Reynolds. Most traditional academies of art, including the Royal Academy, belatedly established at London in 1768, were founded on the principal that only Nature itself and an approved canon of artists were fit for imitation. During the nineteenth century this outlook was revised by the Romantics, who stressed the importance of imagination, and the Pre-Raphaelites, who prized Medieval art for its sincerity and 'truth to nature'. The pre-eminence of the Old Masters was central to the outlook of the first public art galleries founded during the late eighteenth and early nineteenth centuries, such as the Musée du Louvre in Paris and the National Gallery in London. The progressive erosion of this consensus during the nineteenth century was a major factor in the foundation of separate galleries for modern art at the Musée du Luxembourg in 1818 and the Tate Gallery in 1897.

Vasari's personal sympathies are clear in his *Lives of the Artists*, which emphasises the primacy of drawing and the Florentine contribution to Renaissance art at the expense of the more painterly approach of the Venetian school. The latter was transformed and effectively refounded during the later fifteenth and early sixteenth centuries by the Bellini family and their numerous students, including Cima and Montagna. Giovanni Bellini remained an influence on the High Renaissance masters Giorgione and Titian. By 1500 the study of Classical antiquities formed an essential part of the training of any ambitious young Italian painter. The Bolognese Amico Aspertini visited Rome on more than one occasion, as is indicated by his sketchbooks filled with drawings after Classical monuments. Vasari found Aspertini's expressive and highly charged style incompatible with his notion of artistic decorum and characterised him as an eccentric who ultimately lapsed into insanity. Following the example of his master Jan van Scorel, who briefly succeeded Raphael as Conservator of the Belvedere in 1522-4, the Dutch painter Maerten van Heemskerck spent the years 1532-5 in Rome making copious sketches after Antique remains. The extrovert Classicism of his mythological subjects contrasts with the solemn monumentality of his portraits. While both Aspertini and Heemskerck could be loosely characterised as 'Mannerist' painters, their eclectic styles totally lack the cultivated 'Maniera' praised by Vasari and exemplified by the Florentine court artist Agnolo Bronzino and his pupil Alessandro Allori.

Seventeenth-century art was heir to the Renaissance, but it animated the impassive calm of the earlier period with a sense of time and motion. This is apparent even in the 'High Baroque Classicism' of the Roman painter Andrea Sacchi, whose forms are enlivened by rich, warm colours and vibrant brushwork. The new dynamism attained its ultimate expression in the complex, sweeping compositions of Sir Peter Paul Rubens, who travelled extensively before returning to his home town of Antwerp as court painter to the Spanish governors of the Netherlands. His numerous commissions, as far afield as England, France, Italy, Spain and Bavaria, helped to define the European scope of Baroque art. The French painters Nicolas Poussin and Claude Lorrain, who spent most of their working lives in Rome, also contributed to this process. The clarity of Poussin's style builds upon Sacchi's Classicism and provides an antithesis to Rubens' emotionalism. In contrast with the intellectual and heroic scenes of Poussin, the landscapes of Claude have a poetic and elegiac air. Their great joint achievement was the 'ideal' landscape – marshalling a range of Classical motifs within an Italianate setting, depicting variable effects of daylight and weather and frequently addressing the great narrative themes of ancient and Christian art. This 'canon' of landscape painting complemented that devised for representations of the human body during the Renaissance. Claude's gentle romanticism was more seminal than the epic morality of Poussin. His influence was already apparent by the mid-seventeenth century in the work of such artists as Aelbert Cuyp and he continued to provide the most enduring single model for European landscape painters until the early nineteenth century. Pictures by Poussin and Claude provided an arcadian vision of nature which was also realised on a grand scale in the parks of numerous country houses laid out by Capability Brown and other landscape gardeners of Georgian Britain.

25

26. Amico Aspertini
(*c*.1474-1552)
Virgin and Child between St Helena and St Francis
oil on panel
85.5 × 71.1 cm
This small altarpiece of about 1520 includes the Virgin and St Joseph on the Flight into Egypt in the background. At the bottom stone-coloured figures depict Moses and the Golden Calf, the Virgin and Child and Josiah destroying the false altars. The Child wears a red coral necklace, an Italian charm against the Evil Eye. Beneath his foot is a crystal sphere with God creating Adam.
Purchased 1986. NMW A 239

27. Alessandro Allori
(1535-1607)
Virgin and Child with Saints Francis and Lucy 1583
oil on canvas
256.5 × 167.6 cm
This altarpiece was commissioned from the Florentine Allori by Cardinal Ferdinando de' Medici as a gift for Felice Peretti, Cardinal Montalto, elected Pope Sixtus V in 1585. At the feet of the Christ child are St Francis and St Lucy. Both had a special significance for Cardinal Montalto, a member of the Franciscan order, born on St Lucy's feast day of 13 December.
Purchased 1970. NMW A 37

27

28

28. (i) Bowl, Venice late 15th
century
glass
DIAM 28.7 cm
The Venetian glass industry was
the largest in the world during this
period, pioneering colourless *cris-
tallo* glass to produce spectacular
pieces decorated in enamels and
gold leaf. It exported its products
throughout Europe and the eastern
Mediterranean.
Purchased 1973. NMW A 50,580

28. (ii) Dish, Deruta 1510-40
maiolica
DIAM 40.6 cm
Deruta, a small town south of Per-
ugia, was a centre of maiolica production during the Renaissance,
and in the early 16th century
specialised in dishes decorated with
iridescent lustre applied over a
blue-painted design in a third
firing.
Purchased 1969. NMW A 30,141

29. Maerten van Heemskerck
(1498-1574)
Portrait of a Woman
oil on panel
40.5 × 33 cm
Maerten van Heemskerck studied
and lived at Haarlem in the
Netherlands, except for a three-
year sojourn in Rome. In this work
of about 1540 and its pendant *Portrait of a Man* the shimmering landscape backgrounds are reminiscent
of ancient Roman wall paintings.
They provide a dramatic foil to the
realistic likenesses of the sitters.
Purchased 1985. NMW A 235

29

30

30. Andrea Sacchi (1599-1661)
Hagar and the Angel
oil on canvas
75.6 × 92 cm
Hagar, Abraham's mistress, was
expelled by him at the insistence of
his wife Sarah. When she and her
son Ishmael faced death from thirst
an angel of the Lord appeared and
pointed out water. This lucid composition was painted in the early
1630s for Cardinal Antonio
Barberini. Sacchi upheld the Classical tradition of Raphael against
the newer Baroque style in Rome.
Purchased 1971. NMW A 9

31. Sir Peter Paul Rubens
(1577-1640) **and workshop**
Romulus appearing to Julius Proculus
gouache on paper
280.2 × 189.5 cm
This is one of a cycle of four
tapestry cartoons of the story of
Romulus, attributed to the Flemish
master Rubens since 1650 when
they were in the collection of Cardinal Cesare Monti in Milan. After
Romulus's mysterious disap-
pearance the senator Julius Proculus claimed that he had appeared
and prophesied that Rome would
be the capital of the world. The
composition of this cartoon was
reversed when woven as a tapestry.
Purchased 1979. NMW A 229

31

32

Roman and Greek antiquities such as the *Jenkins vase* were enthusiastically studied, collected and restored throughout the three centuries between the Renaissance and the Enlightenment. Together with the Christian themes inherited from the Middle Ages the Classical tradition probably remains the central unifying thread in European art. However between the sixteenth and eighteenth centuries artists greatly expanded their range of subject-matter to include different sorts of portraiture, urban and rural scenes, still life, flower and animal compositions and a wide range of landscape types, including interiors and marine views. Beginning in the Low Countries, painters increasingly concentrated on one or another of these areas. The realistic peasant and low-life scenes of the Le Nain family, developing a theme pioneered by Dutch and Flemish artists, are typical of this trend. A century later the Venetian views of Canaletto demonstrate a comparable specialisation. Academic theory included a hierarchy of subject-matter, in which history painting occupied the most exalted position, followed by landscape and portraiture through to the lowly categories of genre and still-life painting. Although this outlook retained widespread currency, during the nineteenth century the lead was increasingly taken by artists from outside the academies using subjects and working methods beyond the official curriculum.

32. Nicolas Poussin (1594-1665)
The finding of Moses 1651
oil on canvas
117 × 178.2 cm
When Pharaoh ordered the killing of all boys born to the Israelites, Moses was hidden by his mother in a basket of bulrushes on the River Nile. There he was discovered and adopted by Pharaoh's daughter. To the right is a personification of the Nile. This painting was commissioned by Reynon, a silk merchant of Lyon, and subsequently belonged to Clive of India (1725-74), from whom it was inherited by the Earls of Powis. Purchased jointly with the National Gallery, London, 1988.
NMW A 1

33

34

33. Nicolas Poussin (1594-1665)
Landscape with the body of Phocion carried out of Athens 1648
oil on canvas
114 × 175 cm
Phocion (402-317 BC) was an Athenian general and statesman famous for his moral rectitude, who was falsely accused of treason and executed. This painting is one of a pair. The other (in the Walker Art Gallery, Liverpool) depicts the collection of his ashes. The tragedy of his death is contrasted with the daily activities of the Athenians, indifferent to the former hero's fate, depicted in exquisite detail in the background.
Lent by the Earl of Plymouth.
NMW A (L) 480

34. Claude Lorrain (1600-82)
Landscape with St Philip baptising the eunuch 1678
oil on canvas
84.5 × 140.5 cm
Returning from Jerusalem to Ethiopia the apostle Philip met and converted a court eunuch. This picture and its companion-piece, *Christ appearing to Mary Magdalene on Easter Morning* (in the Städelsches Kunstinstitut und Städtische Galerie, Frankfurt), were painted for Cardinal Fabrizio Spada. St Philip's missionary role paralleled the cardinal's efforts to combat Protestantism. Both pictures depict contrasting times of day: here early evening, in the other early morning.
Purchased 1982. NMW A 4

35. Aelbert Cuyp (1620-91)
Landscape with Ubbergen Castle
oil on panel
42.5 × 51.4 cm
Trained and active in Dordrecht, Cuyp was one of the principal Dutch landscape painters of the 17th century. His rolling landscapes bathed in golden light earned him the title of 'the Dutch Claude'. This picture probably dates from the mid 1650s and was already in Britain during the 18th century. The castle in the background, demolished in 1712, was near Nijmegen on the Rhine.
Purchased 1963. NMW A 23

36. Mathieu Le Nain (1607-77)
A quarrel
oil on canvas
73.1 × 90.8 cm
The brothers Mathieu, Antoine and Louis Le Nain ran a joint workshop in Paris. Most Le Nain compositions are suffused with calm. Unusually this painting of about 1640 depicts a violent disagreement over the game being played on the drum head. The young man at the left brandishes a dagger while the older soldier draws his sword as he turns to face his assailant.
Presented by HM Government 1968. NMW A 27

35

36

37

37. Antonio Canaletto
(1697-1768)
The Bacino di San Marco: looking north
oil on canvas
141 × 152.5 cm
Canaletto was the first great Venetian view painter. His work was much sought after by British visitors to Venice and he spent the years 1746-55 in England. This picture shows the view from the Giudecca island towards the principal public buildings of Venice: the Doge's Palace, St Mark's Basilica, the Campanile and the Old Library. It probably dates from around 1730.
Purchased 1957. NMW A 76

38

38. Plate, Venice 1741
opaque glass
DIAM 22.3 cm
This plate is painted with a view of
the Grand Canal from the Chiesa
degli Scalzi to the Fondamenta
della Croce, based upon an
engraving by Antonio Visentini
after Canaletto, published in 1735.
It belonged to a group bought by
the 9th Earl of Lincoln, who visited
Venice in 1741. Similar plates were
acquired by his fellow tourists,
Horace Walpole and John Shute.
Given by F. E. Andrews 1940. NMW
A 50,513

39. David Le Marchand
(1674-1726)
*Miracle of the Man with the Withered
Hand*
ivory
13.7 × 20.6 cm
This Huguenot sculptor was born
in Dieppe, emigrated to Edinburgh
by 1696 and had moved to London
by 1705. He specialised in ivory
carving, producing medallion portraits and a few figure sculptures,
this one a masterpiece of under-
cutting.
Given by F. E. Andrews 1932. NMW
A 50,573

40. Roman 1st century BC and
Italian, late 18th century
The Jenkins vase
marble
H 172.1 cm
The body of the vase is made from
a round Roman altar first recorded
at Pozzuoli, near Naples, in 1489.
A drawing in the British Museum
shows it before its transformation
into a vase in the 18th century.
The subject of the relief is the mar-
riage of Paris, son of Priam of
Troy, to Helen. Thomas Jenkins
(1720-98), a painter, banker and
dealer in Classical antiquities based
in Rome, probably bought this
work in Naples in 1769.
Purchased 1976. NMW A 14

39

40

3. Richard Wilson and Thomas Jones in Italy and Wales

Richard Wilson and his student Thomas Jones were the most distinguished Welsh artists of the eighteenth century, both making a unique contribution to the development of landscape painting. Wilson was born around 1713, the third son of the rector of Penegoes in Montgomeryshire. His father was an Oxford graduate and, as a clergyman, closely allied to the local squirearchy. Coming from this background Wilson received a much more thorough classical education than was usual for painters of the day and might himself have gone to university but for the death of his father in 1728. The following year, with the support of his kinsman the wealthy landowner Sir George Wynne, he was apprenticed to the London portraitist Thomas Wright. During the late 1730s and 1740s he worked mainly as a portrait painter in London.

In 1750 Wilson left for Venice where the artist Francesco Zuccarelli encouraged him to concentrate on landscape views, a Venetian genre popular with British collectors. At the end of 1751 he moved on to Rome where he produced imaginative landscapes influenced by the Venetians Zuccarelli and Marco Ricci, the French expatriate Claude-Joseph Vernet and the Rome-based masters of the previous century Salvator Rosa and Gaspard Dughet. He sketched extensively, both Classical remains and more widely from nature. A watershed in Wilson's development occurred when he was drawn to the compositions of Poussin and utterly captivated by those of Claude. Building on these rich experiences by 1754 he had himself become a Classical landscape painter in the Grand Style. This was a field of art especially prized by the British aristocracy, schooled on the Grand Tour, who enthusiastically collected the landscapes of the seventeenth-century Roman masters and their followers.

In Rome Wilson had associated with visiting English aristocrats from whom he obtained several commissions. In anticipation of their continued support he returned to London around 1756. Like William Hogarth, who argued for the use of modern moral subject-matter, or Joshua Reynolds, who sought to reconcile portraiture with the Grand Style, Wilson had to contend with the widespread British tendency to disparage native talent in favour of foreign artists. In 1768 he was a founder-member of the Royal Academy, an institution expressly intended to elevate the status of British artists. He provided a conspicuous display of his erudition with a large canvas of a story from Ovid, *The destruction of the children of Niobe* now in the Yale Center for British Art, New Haven. First exhibited in 1760, it was a critical success, reproduced as a best-selling engraving and purchased by the artist's first and only royal patron, George III's uncle the Duke of Cumberland. Although Wilson had demonstrated his ability to compose a Classical landscape with a lofty theme, redolent of Gaspard Dughet, Poussin and Claude, he was generally unsuccessful in attracting the noble patronage to which he aspired. It is telling that of the fifty British gentlemen who by 1777 owned over a quarter of Claude's total output, only three also acquired paintings by Wilson.

Wilson was more successful with landscapes of less elevated

41

41. Anton Raphael Mengs (1728-79)
Richard Wilson
oil on canvas
85 × 74.9 cm
Mengs revived the tradition of Raphael and his strict Classicism was profoundly influential. This portrait was painted in Rome, where Wilson lived in 1752-6. He is portrayed in the rich but casual attire of a gentleman at work on a landscape. Although a founder-member of the Royal Academy, he lacked patronage and died in poverty.
Given by The National Art-Collections Fund 1947. NMW A 113

42. Richard Wilson (1713-82)
Landscape with Banditti: the murder
oil on canvas
69.8 × 95.9 cm
The exaggerated gestures of the powerful murderer about to stab his pleading victim recall the theatre rather than real life. This is heightened by the dramatic mountainous landscape modelled on the work of Salvator Rosa, whose pictures were highly regarded by 18th-century connoisseurs.
Purchased 1953. NMW A 69

42

character. His views of landed estates provided a more atmospheric, but equally Italianate, alternative to the meticulous views of country houses produced by Canaletto during his English sojourn in 1746-55. He also turned to the dramatic scenery of his native Wales, which was increasingly appreciated from the 1750s by the antiquarians of the Celtic Revival and the theoreticians of the Picturesque movement. By applying the compositional principles of the Classical landscape and subtly rearranging motifs for optimum effect, Wilson ennobled a wide range of settings, from the gardens of Thames villas to the vertiginous peaks of Snowdonia. Such paintings were especially popular in Wales, where Wilson's patrons included William Vaughan of Corsygedol, the first 'Chief President' of the Honourable Society of Cymmrodorion, and Sir Watkin Williams Wynn, probably the richest Welshman of the day. Wilson's health collapsed during the 1770s and he was appointed to the sinecure post of Librarian of the Royal

Academy in 1776 before returning to Wales in 1781. His reputation survived this melancholy decline and during the nineteenth century even so generally hostile a critic as John Ruskin conceded: 'with Richard Wilson the history of sincere landscape art founded on a meditative love of nature begins in England'.

Thomas Jones came from a background comparable in many respects to that of Richard Wilson. He was born in 1742 at Cefnllys in Radnorshire, the second son of a squire of the same name who later moved to Pencerrig, near Builth Wells. With the intention of taking holy orders Jones matriculated at Jesus College, Oxford in 1759, but left without a degree two years later following the death of the great uncle who had been financing his education. In 1761 he entered Shipley's drawing school in London and in 1763 paid fifty guineas to become Richard Wilson's pupil for two years. During the first year, according to his own account, he was 'confined entirely to making Drawings with black and White Chalks on paper of a Middle Tint … to

43. Richard Wilson (1713-82)
Rome and the Ponte Molle, 1754
oil on canvas
97.2 × 133.3 cm
The view of Rome from the Ponte Molle was much admired in the 18th century. Near the bridge is the 15th-century watch-tower. On the hillside to the right is the Villa Madama and in the distance are the dome of St Peter's, the Castel Sant'Angelo and other famous landmarks. Wilson has adjusted their position so that more can be seen than in reality, creating an ideal landscape following the principles of Claude.
Purchased 1950. NMW A 70

43

44. Richard Wilson (1713-82)
Caernarvon Castle
oil on canvas
61 × 123.2 cm
Caernarvon Castle, the birthplace of the first Prince of Wales, was built by Edward I in the 13th century. In this view, probably dating from the early 1760s, the landscape has been rearranged to create a balanced, frieze-like composition. The theme is the transience of human achievement. In front of this decayed symbol of oppression a mother and her children play.
Purchased 1913. NMW A 73

45. Richard Wilson (1713-82)
Dolbadarn Castle
oil on canvas
92.7 × 125.7 cm
The landscape around this castle of Llewelyn the Great has been judiciously altered to construct a Classical composition in the manner of Claude. The elongation of the figures was also learned from this artist. The peak of Snowdon can be seen on the right. This composition probably dates from the early 1760s.
Purchased 1937. NMW A 72

ground me in the Principles of Light & Shade'. Jones also 'copied so many Studies of that great man, & my old master, Richard Wilson ... that I insensibly became familiarized with Italian Scenes, and enamoured of Italian forms'. From 1765 he exhibited landscape views at the Society of Artists. Between 1769 and 1775 Jones collaborated with John Hamilton Mortimer (1740-79), who painted the figure groups in a number of his landscapes. The most ambitious of these is the large painting of *Dido and Aeneas* now in the Hermitage Museum in St Petersburg. Exhibited in 1769 and later acquired by Catherine the Great, this Classical landscape based upon a story from Virgil is reminiscent of Wilson's *The destruction of the children of Niobe*. Five years later Jones turned to the poetry of Thomas Gray for his major Welsh history painting, *The bard*. He was already in his mid-thirties in 1776 when he embarked for Italy, in the footsteps of his master Wilson a quarter of a century earlier.

After passing through France and Northern Italy, Jones made for Rome where he remained for the better part of two years.

44

45

46

46. Thomas Jones (1742-1803)
The bard 1774
oil on canvas
115.6 × 167.6 cm
Jones's major 'historical' work *The bard* is based upon Thomas Gray's legendary tale of Edward I's massacre of the Welsh bards. The last surviving bard is cursing the English invaders before hurling himself to his death from a high rock above the river Conway. In the background appear the bodies of the bards and a circle of druidic stones based upon Stonehenge.
Purchased 1965. NMW A 85

47. Mug, Swansea *c*.1805
pearl-glazed earthenware
H 15.5 cm
Thomas Gray's *Last bard*, a symbol of British defiance of tyranny, was painted by several 18th-century artists. The source of the figure on this mug is an engraving after Philippe de Loutherbourg in Edward Jones's *Musical and Poetical Relicks of the Welsh Bards* (1784). There were similar mugs, perhaps painted by William Weston Young, in the Swansea Pottery's London warehouse in 1808.
Given by W. D. Clark 1951. NMW A 30,118

48. Thomas Jones (1742-1803)
A View in Radnorshire
oil on paper
22.9 × 30.5 cm
As early as 1770 Jones was painting oil sketches from nature on paper. This technique was revolutionary by the standards of the day, when almost all oil painting was carried out indoors, from studies. This sketch probably dates from 1776, the year of Jones's departure for Italy.
Purchased 1954. NMW A 86

48

Between September 1778 and January 1779 he was in Naples, returning there in May 1780 for his remaining three years in Italy. Everywhere Jones went he made crisp landscape drawings in a series of sketchbooks and also kept a journal which provides a fascinating and amusing account of his adventures. Consequently his stay in Italy is one of the best documented of the eighteenth century. Unlike Wilson, who 'did not approve of tinted Drawings ... which, he s'd hurt the Eye for fine Colouring', Jones was an expert watercolourist. Much of his production comprises atmospheric watercolours of famous Italian views, elegantly arranged following the approved principles of Claude and Wilson. These were made mainly for British visitors, few of whom commissioned oil paintings which were much more expensive. Ironically Jones did not consider his greatest artistic achievement, his small oil sketches on paper, as finished works for sale. He had already produced these at Pencerrig in the early 1770s, but his skill in the technique developed apace in Italy.

The little studies of buildings, devoid of figures, which he made in Naples towards the end of his stay embody an irresistible but understated force of vision unique in eighteenth-century painting. When Jones returned to England in 1783 he exhibited Italian views at the Royal Academy but found that 'the prospect of Employment in [his] Profession was dark and gloomy.' Consequently, 'In the Spring of 1787 – My eldest Brother dying, I came into possession of the whole of his Landed property and toward the Close of the Year 1789, I finally quitted London, as a place of Constant Residence – and retired to my Paternal Estate in Wales'. Settling into the comfortable life of a country squire, Jones only painted thereafter for his own amusement or at the behest of his friends. He was forgotten to the extent that when a group of his oil sketches appeared at auction in 1954, their rediscovery was greeted as a milestone in the history of British landscape painting.

49

50

51

49. Thomas Jones (1742-1803)
The Bay of Naples 1782
oil on canvas
102.9 × 156.8 cm
This painting depicts Naples and
its bay with Mount Vesuvius in the
left background and the Sorrento
Peninsula faintly visible on the hor-
izon line. The Castel Sant'Elmo
and two of the ubiquitous pine
trees frame the composition. This
Classical landscape, inspired by
Claude and Wilson, was exhibited
at the Royal Academy in 1784.
Given by Mrs Evan-Thomas 1952.
NMW A 87

50. Thomas Jones (1742-1803)
Italian Sketchbook 29 March 1777 –
9 December 1778
pencil on paper (186 sheets) with
vellum case
18.4 × 13.3 cm
During his travels in Italy between
1776 and 1783 Jones made
numerous meticulous pencil drawings in small sketchbooks. Most of
these are identified and dated. This
sketch on pages 138-9 was made on
13 November 1778. It depicts the
remains of the Temple of Diana at
Baia in the Gulf of Pozzuoli, north-
west of Naples. A favourite resort
of the Roman nobility, it was also
much visited during the 18th century. Such studies were subsequently incorporated in watercolour or
oil compositions painted in the
studio.
Purchased 1948. NMW A 2528

51. Thomas Jones (1742-1803)
Buildings in Naples 1782
oil on paper
14 × 21.6 cm
At the start of his second stay in
Naples, from May 1780 until
August 1783, Jones found lodgings
with a roof terrace in a house near
the harbour. From this vantage-
point he made a series of highly
finished oil studies of neighbouring
buildings which have a remarkable
freshness and immediacy.
Purchased 1954. NMW A 89

52

52. Francesco Renaldi
(*fl.*1755–98)
Thomas Jones and his family 1797
oil on canvas
74.9 × 101.6 cm

Renaldi was born and trained in
London but Thomas Jones first
met him at Rome in 1781. This
conversation-piece depicts Jones

with his painting equipment. His
Danish wife Maria sits at her spin-
ning wheel. Their daughter Anna
Maria stands behind the spinet
being played by her sister
Elizabeth. The man beside her
may be Thomas's younger brother,
the Reverend David Jones.
Purchased 1962. NMW A 92

4. A Welsh Maecenas:
Sir Watkin Williams Wynn

Pompeo Batoni's masterpiece *Sir Watkin Williams Wynn, Mr Apperley and Captain Hamilton* was painted in Rome between 1768 and 1771. Batoni's only known triple portrait of British sitters on the Grand Tour, it cost about £225, considerably more than the artist's standard charges for three full-length portraits. Sir Watkin Williams Wynn (1749-89) was only twenty when this picture was begun, but had been the 4th Baronet of Wynnstay for all but the first five months of his life. He was one of the wealthiest men in Britain. As well as the Wynnstay property in Denbighshire, he had estates in Shropshire, Montgomeryshire and Merioneth. By the late 1760s his landed income, husbanded during a long minority and swollen by royalties on coal, lead, tin and copper, had climbed to around £20,000 a year and was to grow still further. For the next ten years Sir Watkin spent massively on building projects and works of art until growing indebtedness curtailed his activities in the 1780s. Other costly passions were drama and music. He built a private theatre at Wynnstay in 1772, designed by James Gandon, and in the same year spent £204 on musical entertainments, tickets for concerts and payments to musicians.

Sir Watkin set out on his Grand Tour in June 1768, arriving in Rome in November, where he acquired pictures and sculpture from the dealers James Byres and Thomas Jenkins. After visiting Naples, Venice and Paris he returned to London in February 1769 and married Lady Henrietta Somerset, a daughter of the 4th Duke of Beaufort. A silver-gilt toilet service engraved with their arms was made by the royal goldsmith Thomas Heming. Hallmarked London 1768-9, it is in the late Rococo style decorated with trails of flowers and foliage. Heming had supplied a nearly identical service to George III in 1766 as a gift for his sister Queen Caroline Matilda of Denmark. If the toilet service was commissioned by Sir Watkin before his journey to Italy, it illustrates how his taste was transformed by his weeks in Rome, visits to Pompeii and Herculaneum, and his friendship with Sir William Hamilton. In 1771 Heming made him another important piece of plate which was strikingly different in style. This was a Neo-Classical punch bowl designed by Robert Adam. Silver gilt and weighing 195 oz, it is decorated with swags, anthemion, and rams' heads and cost £186 5s.

Sir Watkin's association with Adam was especially fruitful, for in Williams Wynn the architect and designer found a client with apparently limitless resources and a deep love of the Antique. The result was 20 St James's Square, built 1771-4, probably the finest of Adam's surviving London houses, with plaster by Joseph Rose, painted decoration by Antonio Zucchi and much superlative craftsmanship in wood, metal and scagliola. Adam had revolutionised British architecture in the 1760s with a repertoire of ornament drawn from a wide range of Classical sources, which was applied consistently to every element of an interior. He and his drawing office provided Sir Watkin with designs for carpets, grates and some of the principal pieces of furniture. The Eating Room was dominated by a sideboard table, and flanked by a pair of urns on pedestals. Early in 1773 Sir Watkin commissioned a silver dinner service for the house, one of few complete services made in the Classical manner of the 1770s. It was also the only one produced in its entirety under the supervision of Robert Adam who supplied drawings for all the principal pieces. Known as the 'great table service' it cost over £2400 and comprised 33 dishes, 84 plates, 4 tureens, 8 sauce-boats and 8 salts, weighing 3900 oz, together with 16 silver-gilt dessert dishes, weighing a further 350 oz. It was made by John Carter and supplied by Joseph Creswell, a retail goldsmith and jeweller associated with Adam.

Sir Watkin had continued to buy pictures after his return from Italy, commissioning five landscapes from Richard Wilson in 1770. He later bought from Wilson the portrait Mengs had painted of him in Rome in 1752. Other commissions of the period included a portrait of his friend David Garrick as Richard III by Nathaniel Dance, and Reynolds's *Mrs Sheridan as St Cecilia* painted in 1775 for the music room at 20 St James's Square. He also bought heavily at auction, astonishing his contemporaries by spending £650 on Poussin's *Landscape with a snake*, now in the National Gallery, London. By the time the St James's Square house was furnished, his collection included paintings by, or ascribed to, Pellegrini, Luca Giordano, Guido Reni, Guercino, Salvator Rosa, Panini, Brill, Cuyp, Rembrandt, Van der Neer, Van Goyen, Murillo, Gaspard Dughet and Vernet.

Sir Watkin Williams Wynn was one of the greatest patrons of the arts Wales ever produced. He also typifies the cultural duality of the Welsh gentry of the eighteenth century. More anglicised than their predecessors of a hundred years before, their taste was increasingly formed by London and by the European Grand Tour. At the same time they took an increasing pride in the antiquity of Wales. Sir Watkin was the second 'Chief President' of the Cymmrodorion Society, and he supported Welsh charities, defended the language, collected manuscripts and patronised musicans, scholars and antiquaries. He also fostered the career of the portraitist William Parry, the son of his harpist, by paying for him to go to Italy, just as Richard Wilson had done a generation before.

53

53. Toilet service, Thomas Heming, London 1768
silver gilt
H (mirror) 70.5 cm
The service is engraved with the arms of Sir Watkin Williams Wynn and his first wife, Lady Henrietta Somerset, a daughter of the 4th Duke of Beaufort. They were married in April 1769 but she died in July of the same year. Except for the snuffers and tray, all the pieces were marked by Thomas Heming, Principal Goldsmith to the King, and bear the date-letter for May 1768 to May 1769.
Purchased 1964.
NMW A 50,386-50,414

54. (i) Pompeo Batoni (1708-87)
Sir Watkin Williams Wynn, 4th Bt, Thomas Apperley and Captain Edward Hamilton 1768-72
oil on canvas
289 × 196 cm
Batoni was much sought after by foreign visitors to Rome. This composition is the finest of his elegant portraits of British notables. Sir Watkin Williams Wynn (1749-89) spent June 1768–February 1769 on the Grand Tour. He stands on the left, holding a crayonholder and a copy of a Raphael fresco. At the table Thomas Apperley draws his friend's attention to a passage of

Dante. Captain Hamilton, a flute in his left hand, gestures admiringly. To emphasise the three men's love of the arts an allegorical statue of *Painting* is located in the niche behind.
Purchased 1947. NMW A 78

54. (ii) Sideboard table, urns and wine cooler 1773
mahogany, pine and ormolu
L (table) 244 cm
H (urns) 150 cm
L (wine cooler) 86 cm
These were designed by Robert Adam for the Eating Room of Sir Watkin's London house, 20 St

James's Square. His drawing for the table is dated 14 September 1773. The urns and pedestals were used as water cisterns and cellarets for wine bottles. Their paintwork, though discoloured, echoes that of the Eating Room. The wine cooler in the form of a Classical sarcophagus, bears a medallion of an eagle, a symbol of ancient Rome and also the Wynn crest.
Table and urns purchased 1949, Wine cooler purchased 1990.
NMW A 50,510-512 and 50,631

55

56

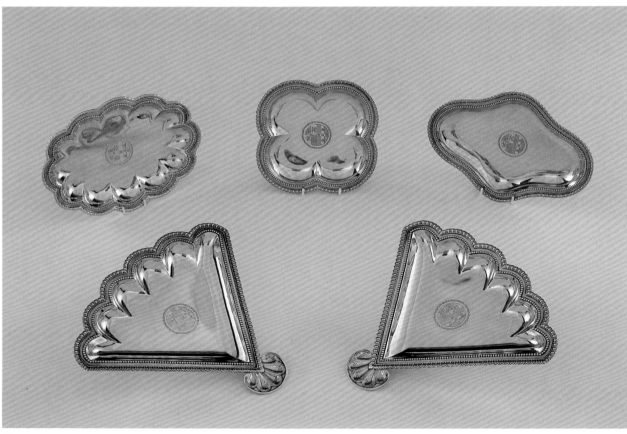

57

55. Punch bowl, Thomas Heming, London 1771
silver gilt
DIAM 40 cm
Designed by Robert Adam, the bowl, described as 'highly finished in an Antique Taste' and gilded 'with a Beautiful yellow coular', was finished in September 1772 at a cost of £186 5s. It is engraved with the arms of Williams Wynn and of the City of Chester and is inscribed 'CHESTER PLATES WON BY FOP IN THE YEARS 1769 & 1770'.
Purchased 1967. NMW A 50,455

56. Tureen, John Carter, London 1774
silver
H 30.5 cm
This tureen is based on a drawing by Robert Adam dated 1 January 1773, which was simplified in execution. It is one of a pair of tureens in Sir Watkin's 'great table service', which together with a larger pair would have been placed at either end of the table and in the centre of the long sides. Its stand dates from around 1800.
Purchased 1989. NMW A 50,509

57. Group of dessert dishes, John Carter, London 1773
silver gilt, fan-shaped dish
31 × 28.3 cm
The 'great table service' included sixteen silver-gilt dessert dishes in sets of four, prominently engraved with the arms of Sir Watkin Williams Wynn and his second wife, Charlotte Grenville. These are again derived from drawings made by Robert Adam in January and March 1773.
Purchased 1992.
NMW A 50,659-50,674

5. Eighteenth-century Porcelain

In 1700 the translucent white ceramic body known as porcelain was made only in the Far East. It had enjoyed an almost magical rarity in Europe in the Middle Ages, but by the middle of the sixteenth century Chinese porcelain was being made to order for the Portuguese market. This monopoly was challenged by the Dutch in the early seventeenth century and by the 1640s hundreds of thousands of pieces of porcelain were flooding into Europe every year, brought principally by the Dutch East India Company, which also imported porcelain from Japan in the latter part of the century. From 1700 much Chinese porcelain was decorated with European heraldry, and several services were ordered by Welsh gentry through the English East India Company. Governments, particularly those not involved in the lucrative carrying trade, worried about the drain on their economies. Despite several attempts to make porcelain using all sorts of ingredients, its composition and method of manufacture remained a mystery. The Chinese had discovered that a mixture of kaolin, quartz and felspar will fuse and vitrify at a temperature of around 1350°C. European pottery was, by comparison, both clumsy and fragile. Moreover neither lead-glazed earthenwares, even when their glaze was whitened with tin ash in imitation of porcelain, nor salt-glaze stonewares were suitable for serving the tea and coffee which were now becoming fashionable, as they could not withstand boiling water.

A passable imitation porcelain, subsequently described as 'soft-paste' to distinguish it from 'true' or 'hard-paste' porcelain, had been made in France since the 1670s. However the porcelain made at Meissen from 1710 was, despite early imperfections, the first European 'true' porcelain. The alchemist, Johann Friedrich Böttger, working for Augustus the Strong, Elector of Saxony and King of Poland, evolved first a hard red stoneware and then a creamy white porcelain. The Meissen factory was formally established in January 1710, with Böttger as manager. Though its wares attracted great interest they were costly and sales were disappointing. When Böttger died in 1719, overwhelmed by technical difficulties and by lack of money, Meissen's future was by no means certain. The enameller Johann Gregorius Höroldt, who joined the factory in 1720, greatly enlarged the range of enamel colours available and evolved a new decorative vocabulary of chinoiseries. These had no oriental prototype and present a fanciful European notion of the East. Meissen also produced imitations of Japanese Kakiemon and other oriental porcelains for the Saxon court which also sold well in France and Britain.

Having discovered how to make hard-paste porcelain, the Meissen factory did its best to protect its secret and to put potential rivals out of business, for example by depriving the Vezzi factory in Venice of its supplies of Saxon kaolin in 1727. The 'secret' of porcelain spread to Vienna, where Claudius du

Paquier's factory was decorating its wares with arrangements of natural flowers from about 1730, some ten years before flower painting was widely employed at Meissen. However it was not until the late 1740s that porcelain factories were established in a number of other German states. Meissen continued to dominate the European market, with agencies in Paris, Warsaw and all the major German cities, and markets in Britain, Russia and Turkey. Chelsea, one of the first successful soft-paste porcelain factories in England, used as prototypes Meissen table porcelains and figures borrowed from Sir Charles Hanbury-Williams, the British envoy in Dresden. Porcelain production at Meissen was disrupted during the Seven Years War of 1756-63, to the advantage of the Berlin factory, but as late as the 1770s Sir Watkin Williams Wynn was buying Meissen dessert and teawares from a London china dealer called Thomas Morgan.

Sir Watkin also bought Sèvres porcelain. The privileged Manufacture Royale de Porcelaine de France had moved from Vincennes to Sèvres in 1756. Sèvres perfected a beautifully translucent soft-paste porcelain and painting and gilding of such quality that it enjoyed an ascendancy over all other European factories until the French Revolution. It was highly prized by British collectors, including the Prince of Wales, later George IV, and the factories of Swansea and Nantgarw consciously imitated Sèvres soft-paste. Hard-paste porcelain was made at Sèvres from 1768, as well as in Germany, Holland and Tuscany. The necessary recipes and kiln specifications were published in 1771, and the latter part of the eighteenth century saw an increasingly free exchange of labour and information, though as late as 1812 the director of Sèvres had difficulty gaining admission to the Meissen factory as a visitor. Many new European factories were founded in the late eighteenth century, most of them catering for an expanding middle-class market, but the manufacturing process remained largely unindustrialised. Coal was not used at Meissen until 1839.

Porcelain-making came to Britain relatively late. The earliest factories, all making soft-paste wares, were established in the 1740s but Chelsea, Bow, Worcester and Derby did not come to dominate the domestic market until the 1750s. Some hard-paste porcelain was made from 1768, but a bewildering range of recipes was used until the early nineteenth century when bone china – a kaolin, china-stone and bone-ash body – gradually became standard. Porcelain was an element in the growing sophistication of Welsh gentry houses in the later eighteenth century. There are frequent references to Thomas Johnes of Hafod in the archives of the Derby factory, and Sir Watkin Williams Wynn bought both Derby and Worcester porcelain. Picturesque landscapes were commonly painted on late eighteenth-century porcelains, and views of Wales are found on both English and Continental wares.

58

58. (i) Teapot, Meissen *c.*1720
hard-paste porcelain
H 15.7 cm
Described in a Meissen inventory
of 1719 as a 'teapot in the form of
an old man', this extraordinary
form was adapted from a design by
the French court painter Jacques
Stella, published in the *Livre des
Vases* of 1667.
Purchased 1987. NMW A 32,076

58. (ii) Coffee pot, Meissen
1715-20
hard-paste porcelain, copper-gilt
mounts
H 21.4 cm
This is an example of the earliest
European hard-paste porcelain,
perfected by Johann Friedrich
Böttger in 1710 and creamy white
in colour. There is no surface decoration as the factory was unable
to enamel successfully until 1720.
Given by W. S. de Winton 1918.
NMW A 30,133

59. (i) Teapot, Meissen *c*.1725
hard-paste porcelain
KPM and crossed swords mark
H 12.7 cm
A Baroque teapot form painted in
red monochrome with European
landscapes, a very rare type of decoration used at Meissen in the mid
1720s.
Given by W. S. de Winton 1918.
DW 589

59. (ii) Teapot, Meissen 1723-4
hard-paste porcelain
KPM mark
H 12.2 cm
Painted in enamels with an early
example of the Chinese fantasies
introduced by the painter Johann
Gregorius Höroldt. The decoration
is recorded in the Meissen pattern
book known as the Schulz codex.
Given by W. S. de Winton 1919.
DW 2559

60. Tureen, Vienna *c*.1735
hard-paste porcelain
H 26.5 cm
The porcelains made in Vienna
from 1718 are often of idiosyncratic
Baroque design and painted with
extreme precision. By 1729 the factory's painters had perfected the
deutsche Blumen or European flowers
which are prominent on this
tureen.
Purchased 1985. NMW A 32,075

59

60

61

62

**61. Pieces from a tea and coffee
service, Höchst** *c.*1770
hard-paste porcelain
wheel mark
H (coffee pot) 25.5 cm
The factory founded at Höchst by
the Elector of Mainz in 1746 produced porcelain figures and table-
wares from the early 1750s until
1796. This early Neo-Classical service is painted with Italianate pastoral scenes of the type popularised
by Nicolas Berchem, which circu-
lated widely as engravings.
Given by W. S. de Winton 1920.
DW 2566, 2576 and 2577

62. Plate, Berlin 1769-70
hard-paste porcelain
sceptre mark
DIAM 25.2 cm
Frederick the Great intended that
the Berlin porcelain factory should
replace Meissen as Germany's
principal manufactory. This plate
forms part of the 'Japanese' service
which was made for his palace of
Sanssouci in Berlin and painted
with chinoiseries from engravings
after Boucher.
Given by W. S. de Winton 1926.
NMW A 30,056

63

63. Wine cooler, Sèvres 1772
soft-paste porcelain
interlaced Ls mark
H 19 cm
One of the greatest Sèvres services
of the 18th century was made at a
cost of 20,772 *livres* for the Prince
de Rohan, who was appointed
French ambassador to Vienna in
1771. The 368 pieces included six
wine coolers or *seaux à bouteilles* at
204 *livres* each.
Purchased 1985. NMW A 32.083

**64. Busts of Cornelis de Witt
and Admiral Tromp, Loos-
drecht** 1780-84
hard-paste porcelain
MOL marks
H 23.7 cm
These are from a group of busts of
Dutch patriots made by the Loos-
drecht factory at a time of growing
republican sentiment. Cornelis de
Witt was a leader of the regime
which excluded the House of
Orange from power in 1654-72,
and Tromp was a hero of the great
age of Dutch seapower. Both are
after engravings by Jacobus Hou-
braken.
Given by W. S. de Winton 1918.
NMW A 30,107 and 30,106

**65. Figure of a Chinaman,
Chelsea** *c.*1754
soft-paste porcelain
red anchor mark
H 17.8 cm
Chelsea, founded around 1744, was
the most ambitious of the first
group of English porcelain factories. The figures made during the
'red anchor' period of 1753-7 are
brilliantly modelled, and decorated
with calculated restraint. This one
is identified with the figure called
'a Chinese mask' in the factory's
1755 sale catalogue.
Purchased 1972. NMW A 30,061

66. Two bough pots, Pinxton
1798-9
soft-paste porcelain
H 13.2 cm
The Derby painter William Billingsley operated a porcelain factory at Pinxton from 1796 to 1799,
and was later to be the instigator of
porcelain-making at Swansea and
Nantgarw. He probably decorated
these bough pots, which are
painted with Harlech and Chep-
stow castles after views by Paul
Sandby published in *The Virtuosi's
Museum*, 1778.
Purchased 1983. NMW A 30,097
and 30,098

64

65

66

6. Welsh Pottery and Porcelain

The industrialisation of South Wales from the late seventeenth century brought two art manufactures in its wake. These were ceramics and japanned metalwork, both dependent on the primary industries of coal and iron. The industrialised production of ceramics developed in England during the early eighteenth century and spread to Wales in the 1760s. In pre-industrial Wales the potter undertook every stage in the manufacturing process himself, and he used local clay. The potters working at Ewenny near Bridgend throughout the eighteenth and nineteenth centuries made 'country pottery' of this sort.

In 1764 a Quaker ironmaster called William Coles leased a disused copper works 'for the carrying on of a stoneware manufactory'. The site backed on to the river Tawe and ships bringing white ball-clay and flint from the west of England could unload at the Pottery's own wharf, while coal to fire the kilns was cheap and readily available. The Swansea Pottery was in operation by 1768. Its earliest wares were probably white or drab-coloured stonewares. These had been made in Staffordshire since the 1720s and were superseded by cream-coloured earthenware – another ball-clay and flint body widely made from the 1750s, which was also produced at Swansea by 1771.

In the late 1780s the Coles family went into partnership with George Haynes. Over the next few years the factory was enlarged, renamed the Cambrian Pottery and equipped to make the high-quality earthenwares and dry-bodied stonewares produced so profitably by Josiah Wedgwood and the leading Staffordshire firms of the day. Haynes recruited skilled craftsmen, including the engraver Thomas Rothwell and the painter Thomas Pardoe. He managed the Cambrian Pottery for some twenty years, producing fine creamwares and pearl-glazed earthenwares, which were either transfer-printed or competently painted with Neo-Classical border patterns, or with flowers, landscapes, birds and animals. In 1802 Haynes entered into partnership with Lewis Weston Dillwyn (1778-1855), remaining as manager until 1810. The business continued to expand, purchasing a steam engine in 1806. By 1811 the firm of Dillwyn & Co had about 140 employees and profits averaged £1500 a year in 1810-16.

Lewis Weston Dillwyn was planning to enter the lucrative but risky business of porcelain-making when in 1814 he heard from Sir Joseph Banks of the experimental porcelain being made by William Billingsley and Samuel Walker at Nantgarw, near Cardiff. Persuaded that high firing losses were caused by their inadequate kiln rather than any inherent instability in their porcelain body, Dillwyn arranged that they should move to Swansea. During 1815 attempts were made to strengthen Billingsley and Walker's porcelain without reducing its exceptional whiteness and translucency. Some of the porcelain made at Swansea in 1816-17 was similar to bone china which was becoming the standard recipe in Britain. A commonly found paste is called 'duck-egg' from its attractive green tinge. A hard fritted body with a high soapstone content and a yellowish translucency is known as 'trident' from the impressed mark that it often bears. These proved a failure and Dillwyn abandoned porcelain-making in September 1817, though the stock, valued at £2500, was decorated for sale until 1826. A wide range of shapes was made, many based on contemporary French porcelain. Under the direction of William Billingsley, the painters specialised in colourful groups of garden flowers, which were produced until the 1820s. After porcelain-manufacture came to an end in Swansea in 1817 Billingsley and Walker re-opened Nantgarw, where they made dessert services, teawares and cabinet pieces until early in 1820. Their exceptionally white and translucent porcelain was a fritted body of bone ash, Lynn sand and potash mixed with china clay. They claimed with some justification that it was as beautiful as the soft-paste porcelain made at Sèvres until 1804, but it was difficult to work and kiln losses were always high. Most of the wares fired successfully were painted and gilded in London by the capital's principal china retailers. Much London-decorated Nantgarw is in an opulent late Regency manner, but other pieces are painted in imitation of earlier French, German and English porcelains, which were already beginning to be collected as works of art. Nantgarw porcelain was soon prized in its own right. *The Cabinet of Useful Arts* noted in 1832 'since the discontinuance of this establishment, the excellent quality of its ware has been more justly estimated, and the prices now eagerly given by amateurs and collectors for pieces of Nungarrow porcelain are out of all proportion greater than were originally demanded by the makers'. Swansea and Nantgarw porcelain was included in the Cardiff *Fine Art and industrial Exhibition* in 1870 and there were over sixty private collections of it in South Wales by 1897.

When Billingsley and Walker abandoned Nantgarw they left behind a large stock of porcelain, much of it unglazed. Their former partner, the Glamorgan polymath William Weston Young, tried to recoup some of his losses by selling this stock. Early in 1823 he was joined by Thomas Pardoe, formerly of the Cambrian Pottery, who painted much of it with flowers or landscapes in his Swansea manner. In 1821 several hundred lots of 'Nantgarw China, beautifully enamelled' were auctioned in Cowbridge, and in 1822 there was another two-day sale at the works which were then dismantled. Lewis Weston Dillwyn resumed control of the Cambrian Pottery in 1824 and introduced an improved earthenware body and new printed patterns. In 1831 he made the business over to his second son,

68

69

67

67. Jug, Swansea *c.*1800
pearlware
Swansea script mark
H 24.5 cm
The tiger painted on this jug was
copied from an engraving in
volume one of George Shaw's
General Zoology, published in 1800.
The landscape, which combines
oak and palm trees, is the inven-
tion of the painter Thomas Pardoe,
who worked at the Cambrian Pottery, Swansea from 1795 to 1809.
Given by F. E. Andrews, 1922.
NMW A 30,556

68. Tea caddy, Swansea 1774
creamware
H 12.8 cm
This heavily potted tea caddy is
the earliest dated piece of Welsh
pottery in the museum's collection.
It is inscribed in scratch blue 'alcy
Davies / August ye 21st 1774' , and
was made six years after the
Swansea Pottery commenced pro-
duction. A similar tea caddy in
Swansea Museum is inscribed
'Swansea potwork, 1775'.
Given by E. M. Bythway 1928.
NMW A 30,363

69. Plate, Swansea 1816-17
soft-paste porcelain
impressed SWANSEA
DIAM 21.7 cm
From the dessert service painted
with 'garden scenery' by Thomas
Baxter for the proprietor of the
Swansea porcelain works, Lewis
Weston Dillwyn. This was nearing
completion in September 1817.
Baxter, one of the most talented
china painters of the period, was in
Swansea in 1816-18.
Given by the Friends of the
National Museum of Wales 1992.
NMW A 31,074

Lewis Llewelyn Dillwyn, who was probably responsible for the introduction of 'Dillwyn's Etruscan Ware', a red earthenware printed in black in imitation of Greek pottery, in 1847-50. After 1850 it passed through various hands, producing wares of mostly poor quality until 1870.

The Cambrian Pottery faced competition from three other Welsh factories from 1813. The earliest of these was the Glamorgan Pottery, built by the firm of Baker, Bevans and Irwin on a plot adjoining the Cambrian Pottery. It produced well-potted earthenwares, most of them transfer-printed, until 1838. The South Wales or Llanelly Pottery was in operation by 1840. It was built by William Chambers of Llanelli who held the lease until at least 1868, though he sublet from 1855 to the firms of Coombs & Holland and Holland & Guest. In 1870 W. T. Holland bought the Ynysmeudwy Pottery, Pontardawe, which had made printed earthenware from 1849. The early twentieth century saw a revival of hand-painting at Llanelli, where plates and dishes were decorated with cockerels, flowers and Welsh costume figures. Its last firing was in 1922, ending the story of a Welsh industry which had endured for a century and a half.

70. Pair of vases, Swansea
1816-22
soft-paste porcelain
impressed SWANSEA
H 24.6 cm
The Swansea porcelain works had several talented flower painters in its workforce, including William Pollard who probably decorated these vases. They are among the largest made at Swansea and are somewhat distorted, illustrating the problems experienced in controlling the beautiful but unstable porcelain body in the kiln.
Bequeathed by E. Morton Nance 1952. NMW A 30,910 and 30,911

70

72

71. Ice-cream pail, Swansea
*c.*1816-25
soft-paste porcelain
H 20.3 cm
Some Swansea porcelain was
painted outside the factory, mostly
in London. Examples include this
lavishly decorated ice-cream pail
which formed part of a botanical
dessert service, formerly at Gosford
Castle, County Armagh. The
shape, based on a Sèvres *seau à
glace*, was made by many European
factories from the 1760s.
Purchased 1992. NMW A 31,075

**72. Pieces from a dessert
service, Nantgarw** *c.*1818-25
soft-paste porcelain
H (tureen) 15.3 cm
L (centre dish) 36.2 cm
The porcelains made by William
Billingsley at Nantgarw in 1818-20
are exceptionally translucent.
Nearly all of them were bought in
the white by London retailers and
decorated in the height of metropolitan taste. These pieces are from
an almost complete service painted
in the manner of mid-18th-century
Sèvres porcelain, which was much
prized by Regency collectors.
Given anonymously 1990.
NMW A 30,177-30,212

71

73. Giant jug, Swansea *c.*1830-45
earthenware
H 35 cm
After porcelain manufacture
ceased at Swansea, the Cambrian
Pottery concentrated increasingly
on the production of transfer-
printed earthenware. This jug is
decorated with a spectacular two-
colour print called 'oriental
basket', together with numerous
other printed vignettes.
Purchased 1992: NMW A 31,125

74. Dish, Nantgarw 1818-23
soft-paste porcelain
impressed NANT-GARW / C.W.
21.4 × 30 cm
After porcelain production ended
at Nantgarw in 1820 Thomas
Pardoe, who had earlier worked at
the Swansea pottery, decorated
much of the remaining stock. This
dish is painted with a view of the
bridge at Pontypridd, completed in
1754. The bridge, with its high
arch over the Taff and haunches
pierced to reduce its weight, was
one of the sights of South Wales.
Purchased 1893. NMW A 31,421

73

74

7. French Art from Classicism to Post-Impressionism

Although the origins of Neo-Classicism in France date from the later years of the Ancien Régime, the movement flourished during the Republic and Empire and was firmly established as the official style of the Paris Académie des Beaux-Arts until the middle of the nineteenth century. Its influence was similarly overwhelming on French architecture and the applied arts, from interior decoration to furniture and porcelain. The study of the Antique and Classicising old masters such as Raphael was central to the Neo-Classical curriculum, at the apex of which was the coveted Prix de Rome, won by Jacques-Louis David (1748-1825) in 1774 . His student François-Marius Granet spent most of the period 1802-24 in Rome and was elected a member of the Academy in 1824. Granet's cavernous interior scenes with cool light effects were favoured by Louis-Philippe, King of the French from 1830 until 1848. The central significance of history painting gradually declined after the establishment of a second Prix de Rome for landscape in 1816 and in 1831 the Salon itself was opened to landscape painters. One of these was Jean-Baptiste-Camille Corot, who painted out-of-doors from 1822 and visited Rome several times between 1825 and 1843. From the 1850s Corot creatively developed the tradition of Claude in a series of Classical landscapes which became highly fashionable after Napoleon III bought one at the 1855 Salon.

Following the 1848 Revolution the Salons of 1848 and 1849 were open to all and that of 1850-51 was selected by a Republican committee. Consequently the Realist painters Gustave Courbet, Jean-François Millet and Honoré Daumier were well represented for the first time. To the naturalism of earlier Barbizon school painters such as Corot and Daubigny, the Realists added an element of social criticism. In the work of Millet, who was himself from a peasant family and settled at Barbizon in 1849, political content was somewhat muted. Millet denied being a socialist, observing: 'I want the people I paint to look as though they were dedicated to their station, and as though it would be impossible for them to think of being anything but what they are.' Daumier was a committed republican who for most of his career earned a living by producing satirical lithographs for liberal illustrated papers. This often brought him into conflict with the authorities and in 1832 he was imprisoned for six months after drawing a cartoon of Louis-Philippe as a greedy Gargantua. Although the critic Baudelaire was an early devotee of his work, observing 'Daumier draws better, perhaps, than Delacroix, if you would prefer healthy, robust qualities', he was never able to make ends meet from painting alone. Generally small in scale, his compositions provide an ironic but humane commentary on urban life, championing the lower classes against the pretentions of a vain and venal bourgeoisie. When increasing blindness clouded Daumier's last years, his commercially successful friend Corot put a house in the country at his disposal.

Following the example of Corot, painting out-of-doors became increasingly widespread from the 1850s. A pioneer was the maritime artist Louis-Eugène Boudin, who introduced Claude Monet to open-air painting around 1856. In 1859 Edouard Manet painted the *Absinthe Drinker*, now in the Ny Carlsberg Glyptothek in Copenhagen. This was the first of a series of remarkable compositions which invigorated and transformed the Classical tradition of French art by turning afresh to Spanish and Dutch painting of the seventeenth century and addressing contemporary social issues. Unlike his friend Tissot, whose portraits and genre paintings were highly successful at the Salon and the Royal Academy, Manet was rejected by the academic establishment and championed by liberal critics such as Baudelaire and Zola. In recognition of the large number of painters rejected by the Salon, a Salon des Refusés was organised in 1863. Its exhibitors included Manet, Boudin, Fantin-Latour, Pissarro, Whistler and Cézanne. On account of official disapproval and public incomprehension the experiment was never repeated. By the late 1860s a number of young artists had assembled around Manet. In the face of the Salon's opposition they planned to rent a space to exhibit their own work and that of other invited painters. The Franco-Prussian War and the Commune of 1870-71 temporarily scattered the group, which included Monet, Renoir, Sisley, Fantin-Latour, Degas, Morisot and Cézanne. Consequently the first exhibition of the Société Anonyme des artistes, peintres, sculpteurs, graveurs, etc. did not take place until 1874.

The self-consciously anonymous title of the Société Anonyme reflects the extreme diversity of its outlook. The term 'Impressionist' subsequently applied to the exhibition derived from the title of one of Monet's submissions, *Impression, soleil levant*, and a satirical dialogue published in *Le Charivari* ten days after its opening. It encouraged community of purpose, and the summer after the exhibition Monet, Renoir and Manet all painted at Argenteuil on the Seine. In 1877 the Société Anonyme endorsed this stylistic label in the title of its third exhibition, but when the fourth was organised in 1879 Degas proposed reasonably but unsuccessfully that the term 'Independents, Realists and Impressionists' be adopted. Ever hopeful of the official recognition which was deferred until shortly before his death, Manet declined to exhibit with the dissident group. Out of its eight exhibitions held between 1874 and 1886, Renoir and Sisley were included in four, Monet in five, Degas and Morisot in seven and only Pissarro in all. The dealer Durand-Ruel organised the seventh exhibition in 1882. In the following year he presented one-man shows of the work of Monet, Renoir, Pissarro and Sisley and exported exhibitions with Impressionist paintings to London, Boston, Rotterdam and Berlin. As a result of this gradually increasing commercial success, the terms of reference of the Société Anonyme had become increasingly redundant by the time of its last exhibition in 1886. In the same year Renoir and Monet achieved official recognition through inclusion in the Exposition Internationale of the dealer Georges Petit. The Impressionists' preoccupation with transient and naturalistic effects of colour and light, allied to subject-matter drawn from everyday life, had transformed French painting and become a major influence in the international art world.

The subversion of the authority of the Salon was confirmed in 1884 by the foundation of the Société des Artistes Indépendants, favoured by progressive painters outside the Impressionist fold. Van Gogh exhibited with them from 1888, but died in 1890. Cézanne, who had been included in the Impressionist exhibitions of 1874 and 1877, came into an inheritance in 1886. Freed from financial need he abandoned Paris to work in the relative isolation of Aix-en-Provence and almost ceased to exhibit until a large exhibition of his work was organised in 1895. Van Gogh and Paul Gauguin briefly shared a studio in 1888, but their joint achievement with Cézanne in the return to a more formal conception of painting was only recognised retrospectively. The term 'Post-Impressionist' was devised in 1910, long after all three were dead. From 1886 the Symbolists argued that objec-

tivity was only a point of departure for art, rather than an end in itself, as in Monet's paintings of the 1890s. A movement common to literature and music, as well as the visual arts, Symbolism stressed the importance of the spiritual and mystical. Despite Auguste Rodin's reverence for Classical Antiquity and Michelangelo, his realism was uncongenial to academic decorum. His sculptures frequently utilised Classical subject-matter, but their titles reveal a primary interest in spiritual qualities. Rodin's friend Eugène Carrière was a republican, passionately concerned for humanity. His misty, monochrome paintings eschew colour to emphasise emotional states. To express such elusive concepts the Symbolists were frequently obliged to return to traditional forms of allegory and their work was moderately successful at the Salon. However their fascination with the ineffable fed the increasingly elaborate subject-matter of modern art, just as the discoveries of the Impressionists and Post-Impressionists stocked its formal repertory.

75. (i) Ice-cream pail, Sèvres
1818-20
hard-paste porcelain
H 33.6 cm
Moving away from the formal grandeur of the Empire style to the naturalism of the 1820s, Sèvres recruited the ornothological artist Pauline Knip to work on the *service des oiseaux de l'Amérique Méridionale*. This ice-cream pail, one of a pair from the service, was supplied to the palace of St Cloud in 1824. Purchased 1988. NMW A 30,143

75. (ii) Ice-cream pail, Sèvres
1811-17
hard-paste porcelain
H 33.5 cm
Sèvres porcelain of the early 19th century is often of exceptional quality. This ice-cream pail is painted with cameos of Julius Caesar and Alexander the Great by Jean-Marie Degault. It formed part of the *service iconographique grec*, begun for Napoleon in 1811 and later given to Pope Pius VII. Purchased 1989. NMW A 30,050

75

76. François-Marius Granet
(1775-1849)
The choir of the Capuchin church, Rome
1817
oil on canvas
194.3 × 147.3 cm

The setting is the choir of Santa Maria della Concezione. In 1809 Napoleon annexed the Papal States and the Roman monasteries were dissolved. Granet regretted this and sought to convey the serenity of the abandoned cloister. This was one of his most successful compositions and was painted in several versions.
Purchased 1979. NMW A 481

76

77

77. Honoré Daumier (1808-79)
Lunch in the country
oil on panel
25.4 × 33 cm
This painting dates from around
1868. Unusually for Daumier it
was worked up from a full-scale oil
sketch and is both fluent and
highly finished. Such bucolic scenes
of people wining and dining in the
open air became a popular theme
with the Impressionists. This work
was purchased by Gwendoline
Davies in Paris in 1917.
Bequeathed by Gwendoline Davies
1952. NMW A 2449

78

**78. Jean-Baptiste-Camille
Corot** (1796-1875)
*Castel Gandolfo, dancing Tyrolean
shepherds by Lake Albano*
oil on canvas
48.3 × 64.8 cm
Set in soft evening light this composition of 1855-60 depicts Lake
Albano with the papal summer
residence of Castel Gandolfo in the
background. The dancing Tyrolean shepherds are picturesque but
anachronistic elements in a landscape south of Rome. This work
reveals Corot at his most receptive
to the landscapes of Claude Lorrain. It was purchased by Gwendoline Davies in 1909.
Bequeathed by Gwendoline Davies
1952. NMW A 2443

79

79. Jean-François Millet
(1814-75)
The gust of wind
oil on canvas
90 × 117 cm
Set on the windswept peninsula of
La Hague which juts out into the
English Channel, west of Cherbourg, this scene may recall a
violent October storm which
wrought havoc at Millet's native

Gruchy when he was a boy.
Although painted in 1871-3, it
reveals the enduring impact of
Romanticism. The British painter
Sickert was profoundly moved by
this work. Formerly in the distinguished collection of Henri Rouart,
it was purchased by Margaret
Davies in 1937.
Bequeathed by Margaret Davies
1963. NMW A 2475

80. Jean-François Millet
(1814-75)
The goose girl at Gruchy
oil on canvas
30.5 × 22.9 cm
Although painted at Barbizon in
1854-6 this scene was inspired by a
visit which Millet made to his
birthplace in the summer of 1854.
Behind the goose girl the geese are
watering in a stream which runs
down the steep hillside to the sea.
The houses of Gruchy, a hamlet
near Cherbourg, are visible in the
left background. This highly finished pastoral scene is of a type
which was highly popular with
British collectors. Acquired by J.
McGavin of Glasgow in 1878, it
was purchased by Gwendoline
Davies in 1909.
Bequeathed by Gwendoline Davies
1952. NMW A 2479

80

81

81. James Tissot (1836-1902)
Bad news (The parting) 1872
oil on canvas
68.6 × 91.4 cm
Born in Nantes, Tissot studied in
Paris and spent the years 1871-82
in England. He occupies a place in
the British 'Modern Life' genre
movement, as well as a position on
the fringes of French Impressionism. This is one of a series of pictures inspired by 18th-century
British art, which rearrange cos-
tumed models and props before a
landscape viewed through a bay
window. In 1874 Tissot had such a
bay window installed in his
London studio.
Bequeathed by William Menelaus
1882. NMW A 184

82. Berthe Morisot (1841-95)
At Bougival 1882
oil on canvas
59.6 × 73 cm
Morisot was deeply influenced by
Manet, whose brother Eugène she
married in 1874. The same year
she exhibited in the first Impressionist Exhibition. This scene was
painted *en plein air* at Bougival,
west of Paris, where the artist
stayed during the summers of 1881
and 1882. The sitters are probably
her daughter Julie, born in 1878,
and her maid Paisie.
Bequeathed by Margaret Davies
1963. NMW A 2491

83. Edouard Manet (1832-83)
Argenteuil, boat (study) 1874
oil on canvas
59 × 81.3 cm
Manet painted this study out of
doors at the resort of Argenteuil,
down the Seine from Paris. In
overcast weather three sailing
boats lie moored together, their
masts reflected in the grey water.
In the background two long house-
boats, one white and the other
black, are anchored at the river's
edge next to a row of trees, beyond
which a big chimney belches forth
smoke. Margaret Davies purchased
this work in Paris in 1920.
Bequeathed by Margaret Davies
1963. NMW A 2467

82

83

84

84. Claude Monet (1840-1926)
The Thames at London 1871
oil on canvas
48.9 × 73.7 cm
Monet came to London in 1871 as
a refugee from the Franco-Prussian
war. This view of the Thames
depicts the Pool of London with
the Custom House on the right and
London Bridge in the background.
Brought up at Le Havre, Monet
was fascinated by maritime views
and had preferred to work out of
doors, *en plein air*, since the 1850s.
In 1868 Émile Zola enthused: 'He
has sucked the milk of our age …
He loves the horizons of our cities,
the grey and white patches which
the houses make against the light
sky.'
Purchased 1980. NMW A 2486

85. Pierre-Auguste Renoir
(1841-1919)
The Parisienne 1874
oil on canvas
160 × 105.4 cm
In 1874 this painting was included
in the first Impressionist exhibition.
The sitter was Madame Henriette
Henriot, who acted at the Odéon
in 1863-8. Renoir often used her as
a model. The title *La Parisienne*
indicates that it represents a type,
rather than a particular individual.
Formerly in the distinguished collection of Henri Rouart, this work
was purchased by Gwendoline
Davies in 1913.
Bequeathed by Gwendoline Davies
1952. NMW A 2495

85

86

87

86. Eugène Carrière (1849-1906)
The tin mug
oil on canvas
57.1 × 72.4 cm
Born in Strasbourg, Carrière
moved to Paris in 1869. This composition of around 1888 is one of
several pictures with maternal
themes, utilising Carrière's wife as
a model. Although highly thought
of and friendly with Degas and
Rodin, his reputation waned rapidly after his death. Gwendoline
Davies was especially fond of his
atmospheric style. She purchased
this painting in Paris in 1917.
Bequeathed by Gwendoline Davies
1952. NMW A 2437

87. Henri Fantin-Latour
(1836-1904)
Immortality 1889
oil on canvas
116.8 × 87.6 cm
Delacroix died in 1863. The following year Fantin-Latour painted a
group portrait of his disciples
around a likeness of the master. He
later decided to pay this allegorical
tribute. The personification of
Immortality holds the palm of vic-
tory and scatters roses on the tomb
of Delacroix, inscribed DEL. At the
lower right are the towers of the
cathedral of Nôtre-Dame and the
dome of the Panthéon, the national
shrine to great sons of France.
Purchased 1974. NMW A 2462

88. Auguste Rodin (1840-1917)
The kiss
bronze
H 183 cm
The kiss derives from a group rep-
resenting the doomed lovers Paolo
and Francesca in Dante's *Inferno*.
In 1887 the French State commis-
sioned a larger-than-life marble
version, first exhibited in 1898.
This bronze was cast by Alexis
Rudier, who became Rodin's
founder in 1902. Purchased by
Gwendoline Davies in Paris in
1912, it was included in the *Loan
Exhibition* organised by the
National Museum of Wales in
1913.
Given by Gwendoline Davies 1940.
NMW A 2499

88

89. Auguste Rodin (1840-1917)
Saint John preaching 1879-80
bronze
H 206 cm
St John the Baptist was a popular
subject with Salon sculptors, who
generally depicted a youthful
figure rather than the mature saint.
This pose was spontaneously
assumed by a novice model named
Pignatelli when instructed by
Rodin to start walking. Another
model sat for the head. The bronze
edition to which this work belongs
was cast by Alexis Rudier who
became Rodin's founder in 1902. It
was purchased by Margaret Davies
in Paris in 1913.
Given by Margaret Davies 1940.
NMW A 2497

90. Edgar Degas (1834-1917)
*Dancer looking at the sole of her right
foot*
bronze
H 45.7 cm
Degas modelled numerous figures,
more as an independent explora-
tion of form than a preparatory
stage in the production of finished
sculpture. In 1919-21 bronze edi-
tions of seventy-three figures found
in his studio were produced by the
Hébrard foundry. Originally
modelled around 1890, this figure
reflects direct observation and a
knowledge of Classical and
Renaissance sculpture. Gwendoline
Davies purchased this cast in 1923.
Bequeathed by Gwendoline Davies
1952. NMW A 2458

89

91

91. Claude Monet (1840-1926)
Waterlilies 1905
oil on canvas
78.7 × 96.5 cm
In 1890 Monet bought the house at
Giverny, north-west of Paris, where
he lived for the rest of his life. In
1893 he purchased a large pond
nearby, which he transformed into
a water garden. From 1899 he
became increasingly fascinated by
the pond, its footbridge and the
waterlilies (*nymphéas*) floating on its
surface. This is one of three works
from Monet's second series of
Waterlilies purchased by Gwendoline Davies in Paris in 1913.
Bequeathed by Gwendoline Davies
1952. NMW A 2484

92. Claude Monet (1840-1926)
*Rouen Cathedral: setting sun
(Symphony in grey and pink)* 1892-94
oil on canvas
99 × 63.5 cm
Monet began his series of over
thirty views of Rouen Cathedral in
February 1892. He returned in
February 1893 and completed it at
Giverny in 1893-4. This painting
of the cathedral viewed by the light
of the setting sun is one of twenty
Cathédrales exhibited to immense
critical success at Paris in 1895. As
a record of the ways in which light
transforms the appearance of a
motif the series nears the limits of
'scientific' Impressionism.
Gwendoline Davies purchased this
work in Paris in December 1917.
Bequeathed by Gwendoline Davies
1952. NMW A 2482

92

93

93. Paul Cézanne (1839-1906)
Midday, l'Estaque
oil on paper laid down on canvas
52.3 × 72.4 cm
Cézanne frequently visited the hills
of l'Estaque, a short distance to the
west of Marseilles. This view dates
from 1878-9 or 1883-4. The
remarkably flat and simply articu-
lated composition recalls Cézanne's
observation that the Provençal
landscape was 'like a playing card,
red roofs over the blue sea ... The
sun is so terrific here that it seems
to me as if the objects were silhou-
etted ... in blue, red, brown, and
violet ... this seems to me to be the
opposite of modelling.' Gwendoline
Davies purchased this work in
Paris in 1918.
Bequeathed by Gwendoline Davies
1952. NMW A 2439

94

94. Paul Cézanne (1839-1906)
Still life with teapot
oil on canvas
58.4 × 72.4 cm
Cézanne painted still lifes throughout his career, but the greatest of
them date from his last years. This
composition of 1902-6 is one of several with fruit, vegetables, crockery
and pieces of cloth arranged on a
table which still survives in his
studio at Aix-en-Provence. The
objects relate to the folds of the
table-carpet-like motifs in a landscape. Gwendoline Davies purchased this work in Paris in 1920.
Bequeathed by Gwendoline Davies
1952. NMW A 2440

95

95. Vincent van Gogh (1853-90)
Rain: Auvers 1890
oil on canvas
48.3 × 99 cm
In May 1890 van Gogh moved to
the village of Auvers-sur-Oise,
north of Paris, where he killed himself two months later. In his last
letter he expressed himself as 'quite
absorbed in the immense plain
with wheat fields against the hills,
boundless as a sea, delicate yellow,
delicate soft green, the delicate
violet of a dug-up and weeded
piece of soil'. The treatment of the
rain as diagonal strokes derives
from the woodcut *Bridge in the rain*
by the Japanese artist Hiroshige.
This work was purchased by
Gwendoline Davies in Paris in
1920.
Bequeathed by Gwendoline Davies
1952. NMW A 2463

8. Art in Britain from the Foundation of the Royal Academy to the New English Art Club

With the foundation of the Royal Academy in 1768 British artists acquired a curriculum, a showcase and a hierarchy. Although the Academy never attained the prestige or the dictatorial powers of its French equivalent, it remained the dominant force in British art from the reign of George III until after the death of his granddaughter Queen Victoria. Its first President, Sir Joshua Reynolds, did much to elevate the status of painting in general and portraiture in particular. This pre-eminence was acknowledged in 1784 with his appointment as Principal Painter to the King, despite the greater popularity at court of his rival Thomas Gainsborough. The latter was a founder-member of the Academy, but he frequently quarrelled with it and ceased to exhibit there in 1784 after a disagreement over the hanging of a triple portrait of the king's daughters. Gainsborough was also an accomplished landscape painter, drawing upon the romantic compositions of Rubens and Watteau rather than the Classical Italianate sources of Richard Wilson. His impact upon younger landscape painters, such as Thomas Barker, was extensive, but his most seminal influence was upon John Constable. In 1799, as a young man, the latter wrote from Suffolk: 'Tis a most delightfull country for a landscape painter, I fancy I see Gainsborough in every hedge and hollow tree.'

In 1793 Republican France declared war on Britain and, with the exception of brief intervals, the two countries remained in conflict until Napoleon was defeated at Waterloo in 1815. For over twenty years it was almost impossible for the British to visit mainland Europe. The tradition of the Grand Tour was broken and painters and poets both sought inspiration in the landscape of England and Wales. Unable to travel abroad and made patriotic by a long war, patrons also became increasingly aware of the unique beauties of the British countryside. These circumstances encouraged the growth of a more truly national school of painting, in which the two leading figures were Constable and J. M. W. Turner. While Constable was more objectively naturalistic, Turner had a wider range and was more susceptible to literary themes and the art of the past. Both shared a dynamic conception of a landscape subject to transformation by atmospheric effects. Throughout his life Turner was closely associated with the Royal Academy, of which he became Deputy President in 1845. Constable only became a full academician in 1829, five years after winning a gold medal at the Paris Salon. His paintings made a considerable impact on Delacroix and the Barbizon painters, while Turner's influence abroad was restricted before the 1870s, when the young Impressionists Pissarro and Monet visited London. Even as Constable and Turner celebrated the British landscape, large tracts of it were disappearing beneath spreading cities and factories. Nostalgia for the past rapidly became a major theme in British painting. This is clearly apparent in the highly personal symbolic language of Samuel Palmer, which celebrates rural fruitfulness and the pastoral simplicity of a world untouched by the Industrial Revolution.

During the first half of the nineteenth century British art and design became increasingly eclectic. The medieval past, initially influential in works of literature and architecture, such as the novels of Walter Scott and the Gothic houses of James Wyatt, became a recurrent theme. This acquired nationalist overtones, especially in countries allied against Napoleon, such as Britain and the German states. The most influential British art critic of the century, John Ruskin, passionately advocated Turner's supremacy over all other landscape painters and Gothic architecture as the most moral and therefore best of building styles. In 1848 the Pre-Raphaelite Brotherhood was founded by three young painters, John Everett Millais, William Holman Hunt and Dante Gabriel Rossetti. Disenchanted with the tired conventionality of the Royal Academy during the early years of Queen Victoria's reign, they sought instruction from nature, fifteenth-century art and subjects from the Bible and historical novels. Rossetti, the son of a refugee Italian professor, was also a poet and his combined interests made a major contribution to the range and sensibility of Pre-Raphaelite art. After the submissions of Millais and Holman Hunt to the Royal Academy exhibition of 1851 received a drubbing from the critics, Ruskin wrote to *The Times* in their defence. Thereafter the Pre-Raphaelites rapidly achieved acceptance, both from the art establishment and a circle of wealthy, middle-class patrons. Millais was particularly successful, being elected an associate of the Academy in 1853 and becoming its President in 1896, the year of his death.

Assimilation of the Pre-Raphaelites into the mainstream of Victorian art swiftly caused the breakup of the original Brotherhood, but it attracted a much wider circle of artists to its ideals. A leading figure in this secondary movement was Edward Burne-Jones. While students at Oxford he and his lifelong friend and collaborator William Morris decided to devote themselves to art. Despite being virtually self-taught, in the 1870s he became the leader of a new school inspired by Italian Renaissance art and a major figure in the Aesthetic Movement, acquiring a considerable reputation both in Britain and France. With Rossetti he was a partner in Morris & Co, the co-operative founded in 1861 to produce well-designed decorative work, usually of Medieval or Renaissance inspiration. Alfred Gilbert had already discovered Florentine sculpture before becoming friendly with Burne-Jones in 1884. The young sculptor rapidly became enchanted by the older painter's poetic imagery. Burne-Jones was sceptical of the Royal Academy and only belonged to it towards the end of his career, in 1885-93. Gilbert was closely associated with the Classicising painter Lord Leighton, President of the Academy from 1878. Like Leighton Gilbert became a pillar of the art establishment. Elected a full academician in 1892, he was effectively an unofficial court sculptor during the 1890s, receiving the Royal Victorian Order in 1897.

In 1877, in what became the most celebrated art review of Victorian Britain, Ruskin expressed faint praise of Burne-Jones: 'the mannerisms and errors of these pictures whatever may be

96. Thomas Gainsborough
(1727-88)
Rocky landscape with Hagar and Ishmael
oil on canvas
76.2 × 67.3 cm
In this, Gainsborough's original religious work, mother and son are shown trudging into the wilderness. With its rich, dark tonalities this picture is an essay in the style of 17th-century painters, in particular the Spaniard Murillo, who was a powerful influence on Gainsborough in the 1780s.
Purchased 1965. NMW A 100

96

their extent, are never affected or indolent.' He continued with a vehement attack on the American painter James McNeill Whistler, resident in London since 1859:

Scarcely so much can be said for any other pictures of the modern schools: their eccentricities are almost always in some degree forced; and their imperfections gratuitously, if not impertinently, indulged ... I have seen, and heard, much of cockney impudence before now; but never expected to hear a coxcomb ask two hundred guineas for flinging a pot of paint in the public's face.

Whistler had been deeply influenced by Manet, with whom he had exhibited at the Salon des Refusés of 1863, and Ruskin's comments provide what is probably the earliest British critique of Impressionist-type painting. The painter sued for libel and although successful at court, was awarded only a farthing's damages without costs, causing bankruptcy. Whistler had shown repeatedly at the Royal Academy in 1859-79, but in 1888 he submitted to the first exhibition of the New English Art Club. This body had been founded two years earlier by a group

of young artists as a serious rival to the Academy, along the lines of the Société des Artistes Indépendants, formed at Paris in 1884. Several of its founders had been trained in France and their allegiance was demonstrated by an alternative title considered for the club, the Society of Anglo-French Painters. The young painter Philip Wilson Steer had studied in Paris in 1882-4 and submitted briefly to the Academy in 1883-5 before transferring to the New English Art Club in 1886. He became one of its most loyal members. An heir to Turner and Constable, as well as Whistler and the Impressionists, Steer was a leading representative of progressive painting in Britain between the 1890s and the First World War. While the Royal Academy remained an influential and respected institution, by 1900 it had become peripheral to the main lines of development in British art. The future belonged to increasingly numerous alignments and groupings of artists whose brief duration and specific aims express the growing complexity and specialisation of twentieth-century art.

97

97. Samuel Palmer (1805-81)
The rising of the skylark
oil on panel
30.9 × 24.5 cm
Inspired by the visionary poet and
painter William Blake, Palmer
settled in the Kentish village of
Shoreham where he evolved a
symbolic imagery celebrating rural
fruitfulness and pastoral simplicity.
Painted shortly after his return
from a visit to Italy in 1839, this
landscape was inspired by the lines
from *L'Allegro* by John Milton,
perhaps the artist's favourite poet.
Given by Sidney Leigh through the
National Art-Collections Fund
1990. NMW A 361

**98. Joseph Mallord William
Turner** (1775-1851)
The morning after the storm
oil on canvas
32.6 × 54.4 cm
Throughout his life Turner painted
maritime scenes. His late works,
with their subtle and profound
observation of the effects of light on
water and atmosphere, foreshadow
the discoveries of the Impressionists. This seascape of 1840-45
and its companion picture, *The
Storm*, were apparently inspired by
the great storm of 21 November
1840.
Bequeathed by Gwendoline Davies
1952. NMW A 434

98

99

99. John Constable (1776-1837)
A cottage in a cornfield
oil on canvas
31.4 × 26.4 cm
Constable developed a remarkably free and spontaneous technique and was a key figure in 19th-century landscape painting. This small but characteristically intense picture of a cottage near the artist's birthplace of East Bergholt in Suffolk derives from a sketch of 1815.
Purchased 1978. NMW A 486

100. Roll-top desk 1862
Oak, marquetry and pitch pine
H 115.2 cm
Designed by the architect John Pollard Seddon (1827-1906), the desk was shown at the 1862 International Exhibition, where it was placed in the Mediaeval Court which was laid out by William Burges. Seddon collaborated with John Prichard in the restoration of Llandaff Cathedral from 1852, and organised an exhibition in Cardiff in 1856 which included works by several Pre-Raphaelite artists.
Purchased 1982. NMW A 50,583

101. Goblet, Jes Barkentin, London 1870
Silver, partly gilt, with semi-precious stones
H 11.2 cm
Designed by the architect William Burges (1827-81) for his own use, the goblet illustrates Burges's eclectic blending of materials and styles in order to produce a highly personal vision of the middle ages, which found its richest expression at Cardiff Castle from 1866.
Purchased 1984. NMW A 50,497

102. Dish, Minton 1859
Tin-glazed earthenware
inscribed MINTON 1859
DIAM 43.5 cm
The dish was painted by the French potter Leon Arnoux, Art Director of Minton from 1849, where he introduced a range of 'maiolica' wares. The central figure of Ceres is from a design by the painter and sculptor Alfred Stevens, the leading exponent of the Renaissance Revival.
Purchased 1987. NMW A 30,162

100

101

102

103

103. Dante Gabriel Rossetti
(1828-82)
Fair Rosamund 1861
oil on canvas
51.9 × 41.7 cm
Rossetti studied with Ford Madox Brown, a close associate of the Pre-Raphaelite Brotherhood. Rosamund was the mistress of Henry II (1133-89). She appears here behind a balustrade in the royal manor of Woodstock. The red silk cord in her hand, according to legend, warned of her lover's approach. The sitter, Fanny Cornforth, was a frequent model of Rossetti's.
Turner House Collection 1921.
NMW A 169

104. Sir Alfred Gilbert
(1854-1934)
Icarus 1884
bronze
H 106.7 cm
Frederic Leighton, later Lord Leighton, commissioned a bronze from Gilbert in 1882, leaving the choice of subject to the sculptor. He chose Icarus, the mythical son of the Greek inventor Daedelus. Profoundly influenced by Donatello, this is one of the finest British bronzes of the 19th century. Icarus was a frequent personification of the dangers of youthful ambition and Gilbert regarded the bronze as a form of psychological self-portrait.
Given by Sir William Goscombe John 1938. NMW A 116

105. Sir Edward Burne-Jones
(1833-98)
The wheel of fortune
oil on canvas
152 × 73.7 cm
This unfinished painting of about 1882 depicts the medieval theme of the wheel of fortune, which lifts or abases man as it is turned by the goddess Fortuna. The drawing of the nudes and the drapery of the goddess reveal the artist's careful study of Michelangelo.
Given by Margaret Davies 1940.
NMW A 206

104

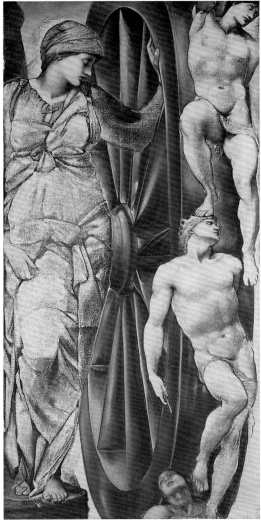

105

106

106. James McNeill Whistler
(1834-1903)
*Nocturne, blue and gold – St Mark's,
Venice*
oil on canvas
44.55 × 59.7 cm
Born in America, Whistler trained
in Paris before settling in England.
He painted this work during a year
in Venice in 1879-80. He later
remarked, 'I think it is the best of
my noctur-n-nes'. The suppression
of details inherent in Whistler's
celebrated night views gave scope
to his aesthetic belief that a picture's value lay principally in the
arrangement of line, form and
colour.
Bequeathed by Gwendoline Davies
1952. NMW A 210

107. Philip Wilson Steer
(1860-1942)
The schoolgirl 1906
oil on canvas
81.7 × 66.8 cm
Steer was a leading representative
of Impressionism in England and
his students at the Slade School of
Art included Augustus and Gwen
John and J. D. Innes. This is the
first of several paintings of Lilian
Montgomery. Not a professional
model, she is here aged fourteen
and dressed in Paris high fashion of
1904.
James Pyke Thompson Benefaction
1907. NMW A 172

107

9. Wales: Artists, People and Places from the Industrial Revolution to the Depression

Mid-eighteenth-century Wales was a sparsely populated and underdeveloped region of Great Britain, still predominantly agricultural and with no cities of note, isolated from England by poor roads and its own ancient language. However its rugged mountains and gentle valleys crowned by ruined castles and inhabited by picturesque peasants made the Principality the very stuff of Romantic art and poetry. Following in the footsteps of Richard Wilson, numerous visiting painters from Paul Sandby and J. M. W. Turner to J. S. Cotman and David Cox immortalised Wales. William Wordsworth's *Lines written a few miles above Tintern Abbey* of 1788 is a milestone in English poetry. Thomas Johnes's country house Hafod in Cardiganshire represented the most complete expression of this Picturesque aesthetic.

By the time George Borrow's travel book *Wild Wales* was published in 1862, both the population and in some areas the very landscape of the country had undergone a spectacular transformation. In Angelsey the extraction of copper transformed the vicinity of Mynydd Parys to a dead, lunar landscape. The iron-smelting town of Merthyr Tydfil was the largest town in Wales during the first half of the nineteenth century. During the great railway age the mining and export of high-quality steam coal from the rich deposits in south-east Wales stimulated mass immigration, forcing the mushroom-like growth of the Rhondda towns and the coastal cities of Swansea, Cardiff and Newport. It was the profits from this industrialisation which paid for the fantastic Gothic Revival castles of the 3rd Marquess of Bute at Cardiff and nearby Castell Coch. In the workshops established by Bute's architect William Burges to supply decorative carvings the young William Goscombe John learned the rudiments of sculpture.

Welsh cultural life changed fundamentally during the second half of the eighteenth century, which saw a new and scholarly interest in the language, antiquities and music of Wales. This pride found expression in the Cymmrodorion Society, a focus of Welsh intellectual life in both London and Wales between 1751 and 1787. Initially clerical and gentrified in tone, this revival became increasingly radical, nonconformist and nationalist after 1800. The two most distinguished Welsh artists of the nineteenth century, the painter Penry Williams (1800-85) and the sculptor John Gibson (1790-1866), both trained and worked for many years in Rome, the international capital of Classicising art. Rather than constituting a nascent 'Welsh School', their training, working environment and inclinations all drew them into the mainstream of the widely established Italianate style. The economic and demographic growth of Wales far outstripped the faltering progress of such rudimentary art organisations as the Royal Cambrian Academy (founded 1881). Nowhere in Wales could an aspiring artist acquire more than a basic training. Consequently although the young sculptor J. Milo Griffith (1843-97) demonstrated considerable talent as an apprentice on the restoration work at Llandaff Cathedral, he was obliged to continue his studies at Lambeth School of Art and the Royal

108

108. Thomas Gainsborough
(1727-88)
Thomas Pennant
oil on canvas
95 × 74 cm
Thomas Pennant (1726-98) was a leading naturalist, traveller and antiquarian. Dr Johnson described him as 'the best traveller I have ever read' and he did much to encourage the re-discovery of Wales. This portrait painted in 1776 shows Gainsborough's relaxed informality and characteristic loose, feathery brushwork.
Purchased 1953. NMW A 97

109. Sir Thomas Lawrence
(1769-1830)
Thomas Williams
oil on canvas
127.5 × 102.1 cm
Thomas Williams (1737-1802) was from 1785 chief agent of the Mynydd Parys copper mines near Amlwch. He was a leading figure in the early Industrial Revolution and this portrait depicts him at the height of his power during the 1790s. It was hung at his country seat in Berkshire.
Purchased 1987. NMW A 451

109

110

110. Joseph Mallord William Turner (1775-1851)

Transept of Ewenny Priory,
Glamorganshire 1797
pencil and watercolour on paper
40 × 56 cm
Turner made tours of Wales in
1792, 1794 and 1795. The last of
these led through Cardiff and
Swansea to Pembrokeshire. This
watercolour, based on a drawing in
one of the two sketchbooks made
on this tour, was exhibited at the
Royal Academy in 1797. Its treatment of light shows the influence of
Rembrandt and Piranesi.
Bequeathed by James Pyke
Thompson 1898. NMW A 1734

111. Anthony Vandyke Copley Fielding (1787-1855)

Caernarvon Castle
oil on canvas
137.1 × 195.6 cm
This is one of the largest oil paintings Fielding ever painted. Probably based upon sketches made
during a visit to North Wales, this
work was exhibited at the British
Institution in 1819. Fielding has
relegated the castle to the distance
as the focal point of a classicising
composition deeply indebted to
Claude.
Given by F.J. Nettlefold 1948.
NMW A 488

Academy. Twenty years later William Goscombe John also left
Cardiff to train in the London studio of Thomas Nicholls.
Between 1893 and 1907 there followed Christopher Williams,
who studied painting at the Royal College of Art, and Augustus
and Gwen John and J. D. Innes, all of whom became students at
the Slade School of Art.

The Liberal Party had landslide victories in Wales in the
elections of 1868 and 1906 and by 1900 the old order of landed
and industrial power, which had previously dominated patronage of the arts and architecture in Wales, was in full retreat. The
first two decades of the twentieth century saw the peak of the
industrial boom. One Welshman in four was a miner and fanciful comparisons were being drawn between the growth rate of
the Principality and the expanding economies of California and
Japan. This buoyant and self-confident atmosphere encouraged
the foundation of national institutions – a federal university in
1896 and in 1907 a National Library at Aberystwyth and a
National Museum in Cardiff. Four years later an imperial British gloss was applied to this burgeoning national identity with

111

the solemn Investiture of the Prince of Wales – the first of modern times – at Caernarvon Castle. Appropriately enough the Prince's regalia and the implements used by his father, King George V, to lay the foundation stone of the National Museum were designed by Sir William Goscombe John, knighted in 1911 for his services to art and the crown.

At this time stirrings became manifest of a specifically Welsh identity or, rather, of aspirations towards such an identity in the visual arts. T. Mardy Rees's *Welsh Painters, Sculptors and Engravers (1527-1911)* was published in 1912 and in the winter of 1913-14 the fledgling National Museum of Wales mounted an *Exhibition of Works by certain Modern Artists of Welsh Birth or Extraction*. Both book and exhibition were expansive rather than exclusive in their definition of Welsh artists. Accordingly men of Welsh descent such as Brangwyn were admitted beside the pillar of the establishment Goscombe John and the bohemian Augustus John. A fundamental problem remained that while the Welsh had a distinctive sense of identity and the landscape, history and myths of their country provided excellent raw material for artists, Wales had always lacked a centralised, metropolitan culture strong enough to encourage and sustain a cohesive school of art.

Wales fared no better than the rest of Britain in the holocaust of the First World War. Perhaps because the social and political fabric of the United Kingdom survived the war largely intact, there was no British equivalent to the anarchic Dada movement which rocked the cultural foundations of Germany and France. In many ways little had changed. Frank Brangwyn, Augustus John and William Goscombe John received official patronage as War Artists or commissions to execute war memorials, while the young London Welsh artists Allan Gwynne-Jones and David Jones returned from the war to resume their studies at the Slade and Westminster School of Art. The 1929 Depression was a more definitive break with the past. As its economy concentrated on the heavy industries of iron, steel and coal Wales suffered even more severely than the United Kingdom as a whole. As the Edwardian dream of industrial 'American Wales' turned into a nightmare, unemployment rocketed to a national

112

113

114

112. Sir Francis Chantrey
(1781-1841)
Thomas Johnes 1811
marble
H 68 cm
In the 1780s Thomas Johnes
(1748-1816) laid out pleasure
grounds at Hafod in Cardiganshire
following the 'Picturesque Landscape' theories of his cousin
Richard Payne Knight. Visitors
flocked to see the Elysium created
in a location previously regarded as
remote and inhospitable. This bust
was ordered in 1811 at a cost of
£105.
Purchased 1991. NMW A 514

113. Dish, Derby 1787
soft-paste porcelain
factory marks
32 × 25.4 cm
The centrepiece of a dessert service
made for Thomas Johnes, the dish
depicts his new house at Hafod
begun in 1786. In June 1787
Johnes sent to Derby watercolours
of the estate, and the 37-piece service, painted with views around
Hafod, was completed in December. Costing £63 it was the most
expensive dessert service made at
Derby in the late 18th century.
Purchased 1991. NMW A 30,223

122

120. John Gibson (1790-1866)
Aurora
marble
H 175.3 cm
In 1842 Henry Sandbach of Liverpool commissioned this figure from the Welsh sculptor Gibson as a present for his wife. Gibson described it as 'the harbinger of the day, Aurora, goddess of the Morning ... just risen from the ocean with the bright star of Lucifer glittering over her brow'.
Purchased 1993. NMW A 2527

121. Sir William Goscombe John (1860-1952)
Morpheus 1890
bronze
H 168 cm
This figure was modelled in Paris during the studentship which followed the sculptor's winning of the Royal Academy Gold Medal of 1889. Goscombe John frequented Rodin's studio and the pose of this figure recalls Rodin's *Age of bronze*. At the Royal Academy in 1891 it was exhibited with the poetic caption 'Drown'd in drowsy sleep of nothing he takes keep'.
Given by the artist 1894. NMW A 2422

122. Centrepiece, Elkington & Co, Birmingham 1893
Silver, silver gilt, gold and enamel
L 156 cm
Given by the people of Wales in 1893 as a wedding present to the Duke and Duchess of York (later George V and Queen Mary), this monumental centrepiece incorporates scenes from Welsh history, views of Welsh castles and medallions of poets and men of letters. Elkington's designer Auguste Willms worked to the suggestions of E. Vincent Evans, Secretary to the National Eisteddfod Association, to produce a celebration of Wales down the ages.
Lent by Her Majesty The Queen.
NMW A (L) 512

123

123. Lionel Walden (1861-1933)
The Dowlais steelworks, Cardiff, at night 1893-7
oil on canvas
145 × 201 cm
Walden was born in Connecticut and studied in Paris, where he received a medal at the 1903 Salon. He exhibited at the Cardiff Fine Art Society in 1893 and was living near Falmouth in 1897. This painting of 1893-7 is based upon a small oil sketch, also in the collection. It is one of several large industrial and maritime views of Cardiff by the artist. His slightly smaller *Les docks de Cardiff* was purchased from the Salon des Artistes Français in 1896 and is now in the Musée d'Orsay in Paris.
Given by the artist 1917.
NMW A 2245

124. Sir Frank Brangwyn
(1867-1956)
A tank in action 1925-6
tempera on canvas
366 × 376 cm
Brangwyn had Welsh parents and his work was much appreciated in Wales. This painting is one of several war scenes from the rejected first scheme for the Royal Gallery in Westminster Palace. These decorations were commissioned by Lord Iveagh as a memorial to Peers and their relatives killed in the First World War. In 1927-33 the artist painted a second scheme illustrating the British Empire which was also rejected and subsequently installed in the Brangwyn Hall at Swansea Guildhall.
Given by the artist 1931. NMW A 2530

124

10. Gwen John and Augustus John

Gwen and Augustus John were as different in personality, life-style, artistic vision and technique as two siblings can be. Gwen was born in Haverfordwest in 1876, the second child of a solicitor, Edwin John and his wife Augusta. Their third child Augustus was born eighteen months later at a guest-house in Tenby, where the family had gone to avoid an epidemic of scarlet fever. Augustus enrolled at the Slade School of Art in London in the autumn of 1894, to be joined a year later by Gwen. Founded in 1871 the Slade was probably the most progressive art school in London. Run by Frederick Brown and Henry Tonks it provided a meticulous training in drawing and encouraged the study of the old masters. Philip Wilson Steer taught painting there, fostering links with the New English Art Club, a progressive exhibiting society opposed to the Royal Academy. Augustus won several prizes at the Slade, including its 1898 Summer competition. The same year Gwen won a prize for figure composition. On graduation, both travelled, Augustus to Amsterdam to see the Rembrandt Exhibition, and Gwen to Paris, where she joined friends studying at Whistler's art school. When Augustus remarked to the great man that he thought Gwen's work 'showed a feeling for character', Whistler's reply perceptively contrasted the styles of brother and sister: 'Character? What's that? It's *tone* that matters. Your sister has a fine sense of *tone*.'

In 1899 Augustus exhibited for the first time at the New English Art Club and had his first one-man show. He was already attracting considerable critical attention, on account of both his evident skill as a draughtsman and his increasingly bohemian lifestyle. In 1901 he married another Slade graduate, Ida Nettleship, and accepted a teaching post at Liverpool University, where began what became a lifelong interest in gypsies. Two years later Augustus met Gwen's friend Dorelia McNeill, with whom he lived in a *ménage à trois* in Chelsea, Paris and a gypsy caravan until Ida's death in 1907. That year he was impressed by Picasso and attracted the first of a widening circle of society patrons when Lady Gregory commissioned him to paint W. B. Yeats. Augustus became increasingly friendly with fellow-Welshman and Slade graduate James Dickson Innes and the two travelled together in Wales and France, painting small, intensely coloured landscapes analogous with contemporary Fauvist art. During the decade before the outbreak of the First World War Augustus devised a personal and romanticised form of Primitivism, both in handling and subject-matter, visibly aligned with other progressive movements in Britain and abroad. This allegiance seemed confirmed in 1911 when Augustus exhibited briefly with Harold Gilman, Charles Ginner and Spencer Gore in the Camden Town Group. The parting of the ways came in 1912 when he declined to be included in Roger Fry's 'Second Post-Impressionist Exhibition' in London. Although Augustus pointedly scrawled 'never exhibited at R.A.' on his submission form for the *Exhibition of Works by certain Modern Artists of Welsh Birth or Extraction* at the National Museum of

125

125. Augustus John (1878-1961)
Edwin John
oil on panel
45.8 × 32.7 cm
The fourth child of Augustus and Ida John, Edwin (1905-78) was born in Paris. After a brief career as a middleweight boxer he became a watercolourist. He inherited the estate of his aunt Gwen and did much to secure her posthumous reputation. This vivid oil sketch was painted at Alderney Manor 1911, when he was six years old.
Given by Margaret Davies 1940.
NMW A 161

126. Augustus John (1878-1961)
Dorelia McNeill in the garden at Alderney Manor 1911
oil on canvas
201 × 101.6 cm
The artist and Dorelia lived in Alderney Manor in Dorset from August 1911 until March 1927. The house and especially the gardens there became an eloquent expression of her personality. This portrait's even areas of colour, sharp contours, absence of conventional modelling and flattened background indicate John's familiarity with the Fauves.
Purchased 1962. NMW A 163

126

127

127. Augustus John (1878-1961)
Dylan Thomas
oil on canvas
41.4 × 35 cm
The artist met Dylan Thomas
(1914-53) in 1935, and introduced
him to Caitlin Macnamara, whom
he married in 1937. This portrait
probably dates from late 1937 or
early 1938 when Thomas and his

wife were living near John's home
at Fryern Court in Hampshire.
The artist recalled 'I got him to sit
for me twice, the second portrait
being the more successful: provided
with a bottle of beer he sat very
patiently'.
Given by the Contemporary Art
Society 1942. NMW A 159

Wales in 1913, by this date he had ceased to feature prominently
in the British avant-garde.

From 1899 Gwen lived in London, exhibiting at the New
English Art Club. In 1903 she contributed to an exhibition of
her brother's paintings, moving Augustus to remark 'Gwen has
the honours or *should* have – for alas our smug critics don't
appear to have noticed the presence in the Gallery of two rare
blossoms from the most delicate of trees ... Gwen so rarely
brings herself to paint.' Later that year she accompanied
Dorelia McNeill on a walking tour of France and by 1904 had
settled in Paris. In 1906 she met Rodin, modelled for him and
became his mistress. In 1913 she entered the Catholic church
and one of her paintings was exhibited at the New York Armory
Show by the American collector John Quinn, who became her
most loyal and influential patron. Gwen remained in Paris
during the First World War, spending the summers in Brittany.
After Rodin's death in 1917 she became increasingly reclusive,
living frugally in the Paris suburb of Meudon. The only one-
woman show of her lifetime was held at the New Chenil Galleries, London, in 1926. Gwen John's pictorial range was concentrated rather than narrow, principally concerned with single
female figures or still lifes isolated by the muted light of the
apartment which she seldom left. In an exhaustive pursuit of the
effects of light and tone she frequently repeated the same motif

128. Gwen John (1876-1939)
Mère Poussepin seated at a table
oil on canvas
88.3 × 65.4 cm
In 1913, the year in which she converted to Catholicism, Gwen John
was commissioned by the Meudon
Chapter of the Sisters of Charity of
the Holy Virgin of Tours to paint a
portrait of their founder, Mère
Marie Poussepin (1653-1744). This
was based upon a prayer card of
1911 derived from an 18th-century
oil painting. Between 1913 and
1920 John worked upon at least six
versions of the portrait, of which
the primary example was installed
at the convent.
Purchased 1968. NMW A 149

129. Gwen John (1876-1939)
Girl in profile
oil on canvas
45.7 × 31.7 cm
Quickly painted on a chalk ground
which imparts a whitish surface,
this portrait of about 1918 is freer
than most of the artist's work. The
sitter was originally painted wearing a mauve ribbon, but this has
been scratched out, perhaps to
concentrate attention on her distinctive profile.
Given by the Contemporary Art
Society for Wales 1947. NMW A 148

128

126

127

127. Augustus John (1878-1961)
Dylan Thomas
oil on canvas
41.4 × 35 cm
The artist met Dylan Thomas
(1914-53) in 1935, and introduced
him to Caitlin Macnamara, whom
he married in 1937. This portrait
probably dates from late 1937 or
early 1938 when Thomas and his
wife were living near John's home
at Fryern Court in Hampshire.
The artist recalled 'I got him to sit
for me twice, the second portrait
being the more successful: provided
with a bottle of beer he sat very
patiently'.
Given by the Contemporary Art
Society 1942. NMW A 159

Wales in 1913, by this date he had ceased to feature prominently
in the British avant-garde.

   From 1899 Gwen lived in London, exhibiting at the New
English Art Club. In 1903 she contributed to an exhibition of
her brother's paintings, moving Augustus to remark 'Gwen has
the honours or *should* have – for alas our smug critics don't
appear to have noticed the presence in the Gallery of two rare
blossoms from the most delicate of trees ... Gwen so rarely
brings herself to paint.' Later that year she accompanied
Dorelia McNeill on a walking tour of France and by 1904 had
settled in Paris. In 1906 she met Rodin, modelled for him and
became his mistress. In 1913 she entered the Catholic church
and one of her paintings was exhibited at the New York Armory
Show by the American collector John Quinn, who became her
most loyal and influential patron. Gwen remained in Paris
during the First World War, spending the summers in Brittany.
After Rodin's death in 1917 she became increasingly reclusive,
living frugally in the Paris suburb of Meudon. The only one-
woman show of her lifetime was held at the New Chenil Galleries, London, in 1926. Gwen John's pictorial range was concentrated rather than narrow, principally concerned with single
female figures or still lifes isolated by the muted light of the
apartment which she seldom left. In an exhaustive pursuit of the
effects of light and tone she frequently repeated the same motif

128. Gwen John (1876-1939)
Mère Poussepin seated at a table
oil on canvas
88.3 × 65.4 cm
In 1913, the year in which she converted to Catholicism, Gwen John
was commissioned by the Meudon
Chapter of the Sisters of Charity of
the Holy Virgin of Tours to paint a
portrait of their founder, Mère
Marie Poussepin (1653-1744). This
was based upon a prayer card of
1911 derived from an 18th-century
oil painting. Between 1913 and
1920 John worked upon at least six
versions of the portrait, of which
the primary example was installed
at the convent.
Purchased 1968. NMW A 149

129. Gwen John (1876-1939)
Girl in profile
oil on canvas
45.7 × 31.7 cm
Quickly painted on a chalk ground
which imparts a whitish surface,
this portrait of about 1918 is freer
than most of the artist's work. The
sitter was originally painted wearing a mauve ribbon, but this has
been scratched out, perhaps to
concentrate attention on her distinctive profile.
Given by the Contemporary Art
Society for Wales 1947. NMW A 148

128

142

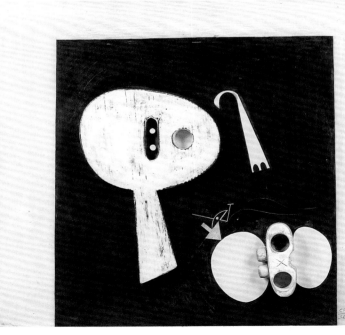

143

143. Ceri Richards (1903-71)
White and dark 1936
painted wood construction
50.2 × 54 cm
The artist was born in Dunvant,
near Swansea, and studied at
Swansea School of Art and the
Royal College. On the frontier
between painting and sculpture,
this Abstract composition dates
from the year of the International
Surrealist Exhibition in London.
It pays homage to Picasso and Arp,
analysing the relationship between
light and dark, form and void in a
similar way to the contemporary
reliefs of Ben Nicholson and the
carvings of Henry Moore.
Purchased 1965. NMW A 221

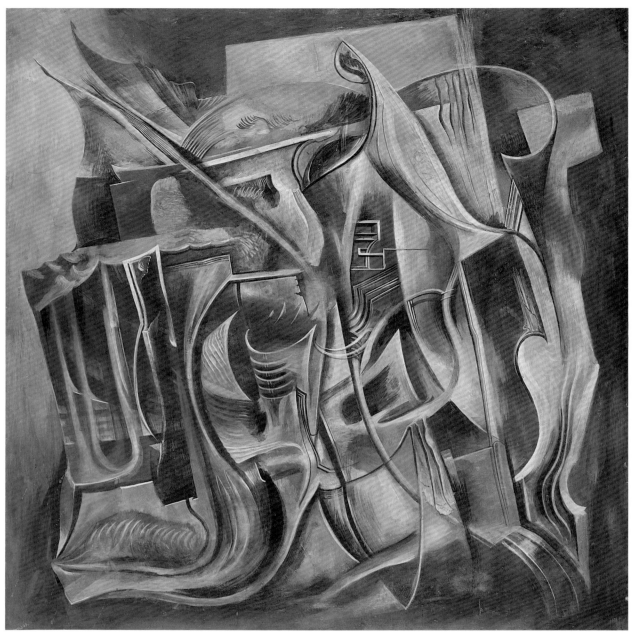

144

144. Merlyn Evans (1910-73)
Beechwood by moonlight 1931-3
tempera on panel
101.5 × 101.5 cm
Born in Llandaff, in 1913 Evans
and his family moved to Rutherglen in Scotland. He studied at
Glasgow School of Art. This work
derives from a drawing of 1930. He
recalled it as 'An abstraction of
lyrical character... During evening walks in Rutherglen I frequently passed by a beechwood.
The autumnal mood and colour of
the picture (as well as the texture
of the smooth silver beech trunks,
and the crisp brown of the autumn
leaves) originate from this
Beechwood by Moonlight.'
Purchased 1963. NMW A 2160

145. David Jones (1895-1974)
Syphon and silver 1930
oil on board
50.1 × 68.6 cm
This work dates from the time of
the artist's closest association with
the British avant-garde, a year
after joining the Seven and Five
Society. Jones excelled as a still-life
artist, but painted few oil paintings. Here the paint has been thin-
ned with turpentine so that the
white ground shows through,
giving the work a luminosity reminiscent of his favourite technique of
watercolour painting.
Given by Mrs Doreen Lucas in
memory of her husband,
M. B. C. Lucas 1988. NMW A 2041

146. Edward Morland Lewis
(1903-43)
The Strand, Laugharne 1931
oil on canvas
38.1 × 61 cm
A view on the estuary of the River
Taf at Laugharne near the artist's
birthplace of Ferryside in Dyfed.
Lewis based this painting upon a
black-and-white photograph, from
which he squared off and transferred the outline of the scene. He had
learned this technique from W. R.
Sickert.
Given by E. F. Lewis 1961.
NMW A 2037

133

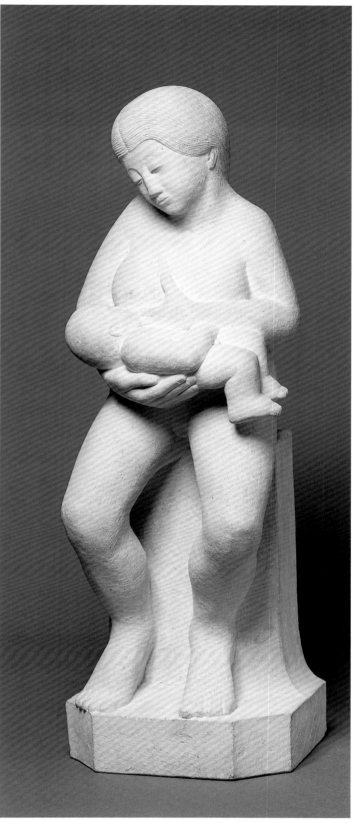

134

134. Eric Gill (1882-1940)
Mother and child 1910
Portland stone
H 62.3 cm
The style of this carving reveals
Gill's study of Romanesque art. Its
subject may have been suggested
by the birth of his daughter Joanna
in February 1910. When it was
included in the artist's first exhibition in 1911, Roger Fry wrote of it:
'has anyone ever looked more dir-
ectly at the real thing and seen its
pathetic animalism as Gill has?
Merely to have seen what the ges-
ture of pressing the breast with the
left hand means, as he has, seems to
be a piece of deep imagination.'
Purchased 1983. NMW A 312

135. Walter Richard Sickert
(1860-1942)
Palazzo Eleonara Duse
oil on canvas
55.2 × 46 cm
Sickert was a pupil of Whistler and a friend of Degas. He visited Venice repeatedly between 1895 and 1904. This view of about 1901 depicts the Palazzo Barbaro-Wolkoff and the Palazzo Dario on the Grand Canal. The celebrated actress Eleonara Duse (1858-1924) lived in an apartment on the top floor of the Palazzo Barbaro-Wolkoff.
Bequeathed by Margaret Davies 1963. NMW A 193

135

Although based principally in Paris, where the first issue of *La Révolution Surréaliste* appeared in 1924, Surrealism was an international movement. The two great painters most closely aligned with its aims and ideals were a Belgian, René Magritte, and a German, Max Ernst. Perhaps because British social and political life had survived the war substantially intact, Surrealism was not formally launched in London until the International Surrealist Exhibition in 1936. At its opening by André Breton, the young poet Dylan Thomas distributed cups of boiled string to visitors. One of the twenty-three British contributors was the Cardiff-born Merlyn Evans. The same year Ceri Richards

exhibited with the Surrealist group at the London Gallery. Himself the owner of a painting by Max Ernst, Richards was deeply influenced by continental Surrealism, although he rather prized his independence from the British Surrealist group. In 1937 Hans Arp, the co-founder of the Dada group, visited the Welsh artist's London studio and expressed deep admiration for his reliefs. Three years later Richards was appointed Head of Painting at Cardiff School of Art, where he remained until 1944. His sojourn there as a teacher effectively marked the inauguration of Modernism in Wales.

136. Sir Cedric Morris
(1889-1982)
Self-portrait 1919
oil on board
38 × 28 cm
Morris was born at Sketty, near Swansea, into a family of prominent industrialists. In 1914 he started studies in Paris which were interrupted by the First World War. One of the artist's earliest paintings, this self-portrait was executed after his move in 1919 to Newlyn in Cornwall. It is unclear if the landscape at top right represents a view through a window or a painting hanging on the wall.
Purchased 1985. NMW A 2156

137. André Derain (1880-1954)
The church at Vers 1912
oil on canvas
66 × 94 cm
In 1905-06 Derain was one of the leading Fauves. Under the influence of Cézanne he subsequently adopted a more restrained palette. This landscape with a Romanesque church and a calvary on a hill was painted at Vers near Cahors in the mountainous Lot region of southern France. Its fresh, self-consciously naive approach pays homage to early Quattrocento Italian painting.
Purchased 1974. NMW A 2161

141. Paul Nash (1889-1946)
Plage 1928
oil on canvas
72.8 × 49.5 cm
Nash saw 1928 as the year of 'a
new vision and a new style'. In
November of that year the Italian
Metaphysical painter Giorgio de
Chirico exhibited in London and
his influence seems apparent in this
formal and austere picture. During
the 1930s it was called *The Moorish
tower, Cros de Cagnes* after a resort
near Nice where the artist had
stayed in January 1925. This sur-
real composition of a fresh-water
fountain beside the salt sea may
have alchemical overtones.
Purchased 1992. NMW A 1663

142. René Magritte (1898-1967)
The empty mask 1928
oil on canvas
81.3 × 116.2 cm
In his essay 'Words and images',
published in 1929, the Belgian Surrealist Magritte observed that each
image 'suggests that there are
others behind it'. Viewed through
a freestanding frame of irregular
shape, these images are a sky, a
lead curtain festooned with sleigh
bells, a house façade, a sheet of
paper cut-outs, a forest and a fire.
The title evokes the fear of the
invisible which pervades the artist's
work and reflects the Surrealists'
fascination with Freud's notion of
the unconscious.
Purchased 1973. NMW A 2051

141

145

146

12. Art from the Second World War to the Present Day

Foreshadowed by such works as Picasso's Cubist compositions or the Rayonist pictures of Natalia Goncharova, abstraction first flourished after the First World War in the work of Central European artists, including the Hungarian László Moholy-Nagy and the German Willi Baumeister. In Britain the first group of abstractionists, Unit One, was founded in London in 1932-3 and held its only show in 1934. That year Ben Nicholson visited Piet Mondrian and exhibited his first 'white relief'. Nicholson had some influence upon his friends in the Seven and Five Society, and John Piper experimented with abstraction between 1935 and 1938. Although the rise of Fascism, culminating in the outbreak of the Second World War, caused many leading members of the Continental avant-garde to flee to Britain, the atmosphere of mounting crisis which ensued was not conducive to the transplantation of Modernism.

The British artistic movement most closely associated with the war, Neo-Romanticism, fostered a backward-looking and elegiac figuration closely attuned to the patriotic spirit encouraged by the Ministry of Information. The Neo-Romantics' fascination with the British landscape was in some respects comparable with that of early nineteenth-century painters, who had been similarly introspective in the face of a national crisis which dislocated contact with Continental Europe. John Piper met the Welsh writer Myfanwy Evans, who subsequently became his wife, in 1934 and two years later made the first of numerous painting trips to Wales. In 1934 the painter and printmaker Graham Sutherland was captivated by the landscape of Pembrokeshire and, finding its terrain endlessly varied and full of forms and suggestions which stimulated his artistic process, returned regularly for a decade. As leading participants in the Official War Artists' Scheme both artists recorded bomb damage and the Home Front in Wales. In 1943 Ceri Richards, Head of Painting at Cardiff School of Art, was commissioned to make drawings of Welsh tinplate workers. The following year he began a series of paintings on the theme of birth and death based upon the poems of Dylan Thomas. David Jones was not an Official War Artist, but the conflict inspired him to produce a series of large drawings of great detail and symbolic elaboration in which Celtic history is a recurrent theme. His conflation of a tremulous present and a timeless past, analogous with the contemporary novels of John Cowper Powys, demonstrated the possibility of a recognisable 'Welsh Art', but in a way too personal to serve as a blueprint for others.

Throughout Europe the devastation of the war cast a pervasive shadow long after its end. In Britain this stimulated such bleak but powerful works as Francis Bacon's *Three studies for figures at the base of a crucifixion* and Merlyn Evans's political paintings. Among the innumerable refugees who escaped to Britain were exponents of the European Expressionist and Realist traditions, including the Silesian Martin Bloch and the Pole Josef Herman. Bloch painted in Wales on several occasions and in 1944 Herman settled at Ystradgynlais, where he initially shared a room with L. S. Lowry. In 1951 both painted Welsh subjects

for the Festival of Britain, held to commemorate the centenary of the Great Exhibition in 1851. Rather self-consciously this large festival on London's South Bank sought to celebrate the past achievements and future expectations of a country theoretically at peace but actually embroiled with a Cold War in Europe and a real war in Korea. Although it was destroyed by a protesting member of the public, Reg Butler's prize-winning *Unknown political prisoner* of 1952 rather more succinctly expressed the spirit of the times. Butler had been an assistant to the sculptor Henry Moore. A friend of Ben Nicholson, Moore had been abreast of the principal trends in Modernism since 1930, exhibiting with the Seven and Five Society, Unit One and at the International Surrealist Exhibition before becoming an Official War Artist. After winning the International Sculpture Prize at the first post-war Venice Biennale in 1948, Moore rapidly became the most celebrated sculptor in Europe. Although deeply interested in the abstract interrelationship between forms, he remained essentially a figurative sculptor. Like his old friend Barbara Hepworth, Nicholson's ex-wife, Moore was profoundly interested in direct carving and the relationship between sculpture and landscape. Ironically his international-celebrity status and the enormous demand for his work made him increasingly dependent on assistants and casting techniques.

As the only major power to emerge from the war comparatively unscathed, from 1945 the United States enjoyed global economic and political influence. Cultural supremacy followed, in the wider terms of language, popular music, advertising, film and fashion, as well as those of traditional 'high art'. During the

147. David Jones (1895-1974)
The greeting to Mary
pencil, crayon and watercolour on paper
77.5 × 57.8 cm
Although born in London the Catholic writer and artist David Jones considered himself to be Welsh and his novel *In Parenthesis* was applauded as 'the first truly Anglo-Welsh product'. This drawing of around 1963 locates the *Annunciation* in a Welsh hill setting. Characteristically it interweaves three religious themes: the dawn of the Christian era; the Annunciation as a prelude to the Passion; and the Celtic myth of redemption. In the sky the constellation of Virgo is juxtaposed to that of Libra, which has the form of a cross.
Purchased 1976. NMW A 2529

147

148

148. Josef Herman (*b.*1911)
Miners singing 1950-1
tempera on board
43 × 122 cm
A refugee from Poland, Herman
spent the decade 1944-54 in
Ystradgynlais where he painted his
best-known works of mining
themes. This is a study for his
greatest painting, the monumental
Miners executed for the Pavilion of
Minerals of the Island at the 1951
Festival of Britain. The artist began
with the figure with an upraised
arm at the left, only subsequently
making narrative sense of its pose
by incorporating it with a group of
singers.
Purchased 1992. NMW A 1674

149. John Piper (1903-92)
*A ruined house, Hampton Gay,
Oxfordshire* 1941
oil and indian ink on canvas on
board
63.5 × 76.7 cm
The ruined manor house at
Hampton Gay is a picturesque ruin
in a desolate spot. Its subject may
have been suggested by the pictures of historic buildings devas-
tated in the Blitz which Piper
undertook for the War Artists'
Advisory Committee.
Lent by the Derek Williams Trust.
NMW A (L) 584

149

153

154. Henry Moore
(1898-1986)
Upright motif no.8 1956
bronze
H 198 cm
By 1950 Henry Moore was generally recognised as the leading
avant-garde artist in Britain. In
1955-6 he worked upon a series of
upright bronze sculptures reminiscent of totem poles and the
statues of Brancusi. Three of these
Upright motifs were sometimes dis-
played together to evoke a Crucifixion group. Here the rounded
humanoid forms set against verti-
cal fluting suggest a figure bound
to a Classical column, such as St
Sebastian, or Christ at the Flagell-
ation.
Purchased 1962. NMW A 2415

154

155

155. Graham Sutherland
(1903-80)
Trees with a g-shaped form I 1972
oil on canvas
117 × 172 cm
Towards the end of his life the
artist frequently revisited West
Wales where he often stayed at
Benton Castle, a 'small but almost
perfect castle' above the River
Cleddau. Here he came upon a
tree with a massive, gnarled root-
formation which provided the
principal motif in this work. The
distorted central shape contrasts
with the symmetrical uprights of
the tree trunks, just as the black
background sets off the acid green
of the foreground forms.
Purchased 1973. NMW A 220

156

156. R. B. Kitaj (*b.*1932)
Tedeum 1963
acrylic and oil on canvas
122.5 × 184 cm
Born in Ohio, Kitaj came to Britain in 1958, training in Oxford and at the Royal College of Art. Surrealism and iconographical studies heavily influence his work. This painting, pronounced 'tedium', has

as its source a photograph of a production of *No Exit* by Jean-Paul Sartre. The giant figure on the right is Goethe, who gazes out of the window. His languid stance reflects the title and refers to *Ennui*, a painting by W. R. Sickert that encapsulates human discontent.
Purchased 1977. NMW A 226

157. Allen Jones (*b.*1937)
Buses 1964
oil on cotton duck
274.3 × 304.8 cm
Jones recalled: 'Throughout my work I've played with devices to convey movement. In this one a sequence of colour juxtapositions allows the eye to shunt slowly across the canvas. The analogy is to the London traffic jams, where basically everyone is moving in one direction but somehow or other it all shunts backwards and forwards because they are all going at different speeds and moving at different times.'
Purchased 1977. NMW A 2178

155

155. Graham Sutherland
(1903-80)
Trees with a g-shaped form I 1972
oil on canvas
117 × 172 cm
Towards the end of his life the
artist frequently revisited West
Wales where he often stayed at
Benton Castle, a 'small but almost
perfect castle' above the River
Cleddau. Here he came upon a
tree with a massive, gnarled root-
formation which provided the
principal motif in this work. The
distorted central shape contrasts
with the symmetrical uprights of
the tree trunks, just as the black
background sets off the acid green
of the foreground forms.
Purchased 1973. NMW A 220

156

156. R. B. Kitaj (*b.*1932)
Tedeum 1963
acrylic and oil on canvas
122.5 × 184 cm
Born in Ohio, Kitaj came to Britain in 1958, training in Oxford and at the Royal College of Art. Surrealism and iconographical studies heavily influence his work. This painting, pronounced 'tedium', has as its source a photograph of a production of *No Exit* by Jean-Paul Sartre. The giant figure on the right is Goethe, who gazes out of the window. His languid stance reflects the title and refers to *Ennui*, a painting by W. R. Sickert that encapsulates human discontent.
Purchased 1977. NMW A 226

157. Allen Jones (*b.*1937)
Buses 1964
oil on cotton duck
274.3 × 304.8 cm
Jones recalled: 'Throughout my work I've played with devices to convey movement. In this one a sequence of colour juxtapositions allows the eye to shunt slowly across the canvas. The analogy is to the London traffic jams, where basically everyone is moving in one direction but somehow or other it all shunts backwards and forwards because they are all going at different speeds and moving at different times.'
Purchased 1977. NMW A 2178

157

158

158. Michael Andrews (*b.*1928)
The Cathedral, The Southern Faces/
Uluru (Ayers Rock) 1987
acrylic on canvas
243.8 × 388.6 cm
Andrews studied at the Slade
School of Art and visited Ayers
Rock in 1983. Situated in the
Uluru National Park in Central
Australia, it is a religious site of the
highest significance to the Abori-
gines and a major tourist attraction. This dual significance is
alluded to by the contrast between
the profound subject-matter and
the bright colours and flat handling, reminiscent of Pop Art. When
he visited this 'magical mountain'
Andrews recalled the famous
Anglican hymn *Rock of Ages, cleft*
for me.
Lent by the Derek Williams Trust.
NMW A (L) 918

159. Francis Bacon (1909-92)
Study for self-portrait 1963
oil on canvas
165.2 × 142.6 cm
Francis Bacon was the principal
figurative painter in post-war Britain. Conditioned by Surrealism, he
exploited the expressive potential
of portraiture and was largely
indifferent to its representational
values. Here the heavily modelled
seated figure seems overwhelmed
by its flatly painted surroundings.
Purchased 1978. NMW A 218

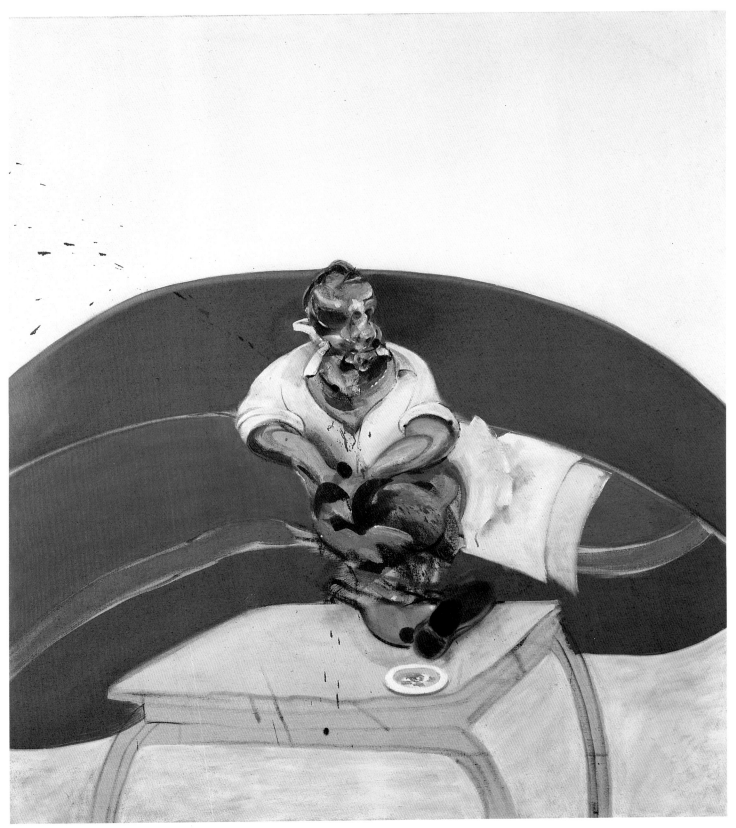

159

160

160. Lucian Freud (*b.*1922)
The painter's brother Stephen 1985
oil on canvas
51 × 40.9 cm
Lucian Freud was born in Berlin, the grandson of Sigmund Freud. His style displays points of contact with the work of the German 'New Realists' of the 1920s, the pictures of his teacher Sir Cedric Morris and those of Francis Bacon. Freud principally paints figures in interiors. These are remarkable for their psychological penetration and passionate intensity.
Purchased 1987. NMW A 223

Further Reading

Introduction: The Growth of a Collection

D. A. Bassett, 'The Making of a National Museum', *Transactions of the Honourable Society of Cymmrodorion*, London, 1982, pp.153-85; 1983, pp.187-220; 1984, pp.217-316 and 1990, pp.193-260

Cardiff Fine Art and Industrial Exhibition, exh.cat, Cardiff, 1870, 1881 and 1896

Cardiff Free Library and Museum (subsequently Cardiff Museum and Art Gallery and The Welsh Museum of Natural History, Arts and Antiquities), *Annual Report*, Cardiff, 1862-1911

Catalogue of Loan Exhibition of Paintings, exh.cat, National Museum of Wales, Cardiff, 1913

Catalogue of an Exhibition of Works by certain modern Artists of Welsh Birth or Extraction, exh.cat, National Museum of Wales, Cardiff, 1914

Contemporary Art Society for Wales 50th Anniversasry Exhibition, exh.cat, National Museum of Wales, Cardiff, 1987

M. L. Evans, *The Derek Williams Collection at the National Museum of Wales*, National Museum of Wales, Cardiff, 1989

J. M. Gibbs, *James Pyke Thompson: The Turner House, Penarth 1888-1988*, National Museum of Wales, Cardiff, 1990

J. Ingamells, *The Davies Collection of French Art*, National Museum of Wales, Cardiff, 1967

National Museum of Wales, Cardiff, *Annual Report*, Cardiff, 1909-78

National Museum of Wales, Cardiff, *Charter of Incorporation*, Cardiff, 1912

National Museum of Wales, Cardiff, *Catalogue of the Pictures and Sculpture exhibited in the Cardiff Collections, Trinity Street*, Cardiff, 1914

National Museum of Wales, Cardiff, *Catalogue of the Gwendoline E. Davies Bequest*, Cardiff, 1952

National Museum of Wales, Cardiff, *Catalogue of Oil-Paintings*, Cardiff, 1955

National Museum of Wales, Cardiff, *Catalogue of the Margaret S. Davies Bequest*, Cardiff, 1963

National Museum of Wales, Cardiff, *Charter and Statutes*, Cardiff, 1991

T. Mardy Rees, *Welsh Painters, Engravers, Sculptors (1527-1911)*, Caernarfon, 1912

J. Ward, *A Guide to the Pyke-Thompson Loan Collection of Water-Colour Paintings etc. in the Cardiff Corporation Museum and Art Gallery*, Cardiff, 1897

F. Wedmore, *A Descriptive Catalogue of Drawings, Prints, Pictures and Porcelain collected by James Pyke Thompson and placed in the Turner House, Penarth*, Penarth, 1900

E. White, *The Ladies of Gregynog*, Newtown, 1984

I. Williams, *A Guide to the Collection of Welsh Porcelain*, National Museum of Wales, Cardiff, 1931

A. S. Wittlin, *The Museum*, London, 1949

1. Art in Wales from the Middle Ages to the Enlightenment

Artists of the Tudor Court, exh.cat, ed. R. Strong, Victoria and Albert Museum, London, 1983

J. Ballinger, 'Katheryn of Berain', *Y Cymmrodor*, vol.XL, 1929, pp.1-42

D. W. Howell, *Patriarchs and Parasites: The Gentry of South-West Wales in the 18th Century*, Cardiff, 1986

P. Jenkins, *A History of Modern Wales 1536-1990*, London, 1992

A. Laing, 'Lord Herbert of Cherbury', *National-Art Collections Fund Review*, vol.LXXXVII, 1991, pp.147-52

K. B. McFarlane, *Hans Memling*, London, 1971

P. Morgan, *A New History of Wales: The 18th-Century Renaissance*, Llandybie, 1981

E. Rowan (ed.), *Art in Wales: An Illustrated History 2000BC-AD1850*, Cardiff, 1978

J. Steegman, *A Survey of Portraits in Welsh Houses*, National Museum of Wales, Cardiff, 1957 and 1962

D. H. Turner, *The Hastings Hours*, London, 1983

A. Wassenbergh, *L'Art du Portrait en Frise au Seizième Siècle*, Leiden, 1934

G. A. Williams, *When was Wales?*, London, 1985

2. Old Masters from the Renaissance to the Enlightenment

A. Blunt, *The Paintings of Nicolas Poussin*, London, 1966

W. G. Constable and L. G. Links, *Canaletto*, Oxford, 1976 and 1989

A. D. Fraser Jenkins, 'An altarpiece by Alessandro Allori', *Amgueddfa*, vol.IX, 1971, pp.16-23

From Borso to Cesare d'Este: The School of Ferrara 1450-1628, exh.cat, Matthiesen Fine Art Ltd, London, 1984

R. Grosshans, *Maerten van Heemskerck*, Berlin, 1980

J. Held, 'The case against the Cardiff "Rubens" cartoons', *The Burlington Magazine*, vol.CXXV, 1983, pp.132-6

P. Humfrey, *Cima da Conegliano*, Cambridge, 1983

M. Jaffé, 'Rubens's Aeneas cartoons at Cardiff', *The Burlington Magazine*, vol.CXXV, 1983, pp.136-51

M. Jaffé and P. Cannon-Brookes, '..Sono dissegni coloriti di Rubens', *The Burlington Magazine*, vol.CXXVIII, 1986, pp.780-5

Nicolas Poussin/Claude Lorrain: zu den Bildern im Städel, exh.cat, Städtische Galerie im Städelschen Kunstinstitut, Frankfurt, 1988

A. Sutherland Harris, *Andrea Sacchi*, Oxford, 1977

3. Richard Wilson and Thomas Jones in Italy and Wales

W. G. Constable, *Richard Wilson*, London, 1952

L. Gowing, *The Originality of Thomas Jones*, London, 1985

R. C. B. Oliver, *The Family History of Thomas Jones, the Artist*, Llandysul, 1970

A. P. Oppé, 'The Memoirs of Thomas Jones', *The Walpole Society*, vol.XXIII, 1951

D. H. Solkin, *Richard Wilson*, Tate Gallery, London, 1982

Travels in Italy 1776-1783, exh.cat, ed. F. W. Hawcroft, Whitworth Art Gallery, Manchester, 1988

4. A Welsh Maecenas : Sir Watkin Williams Wynn

A. M. Clark, *Pompeo Batoni: A Complete Catalogue of his Works*, Oxford, 1985

B. Ford, 'Sir Watkin Williams-Wynn: A Welsh Maecenas', *Apollo*, vol.XCIX, 1974, pp.435-9

P. Hughes, 'An Adam Punch Bowl', *The Burlington Magazine*, vol.CIX, 1967, p.646

P. Hughes, 'The Williams-Wynn silver in the National Museum of Wales', *Connoisseur*, vol.CLXXXIV, 1973, pp.33-7

T. W. Pritchard, *The Wynns at Wynnstay*, Caerwys, 1982

5. Eighteenth-century Porcelain

E. Adams, *Chelsea Porcelain*, London, 1987

R. Behrends, *Das Meissener Musterbuch für Höroldt-Chinoiserien*, Leipzig, 1978

Ceramics of Derbyshire, exh.cat, ed. H. G. Bradley *et al*, London, 1978

R. Charles, *Continental Porcelain of the 18th Century*, London, 1964

C. C. Dauterman, *The Wrightsman Collection*, vol.IV, *Porcelain*, Metropolitan Museum of Art, New York, 1970

W. Goder *et al*, *Johann Friedrich Böttger: Die Erfindung des Europäisches Porzellans*, Leipzig, 1982

E. Köllerman and M. Jarchow, *Berliner Porzellan*, Munich, 1987

Loosdrechts Porselein 1774-1784, exh.cat, ed. W. M. Zappey *et al*, Zwolle, 1988

Meissener Porzellan 1710-1850, exh.cat, ed. R. Rückert, Munich, 1966

6. Welsh Pottery and Porcelain

R. J. Charleston *et al*, *English Porcelain 1745-1850*, London, 1965

G. Hughes and R. Pugh, *Llanelly Pottery*, Llanelli, 1990

P. Hughes, *Welsh China*, National Museum of Wales, Cardiff, 1972

E. Jenkins, *Swansea Porcelain*, Cowbridge, 1970

W. Grant Davidson, 'Early Swansea Pottery, 1764-1810', *Transactions of the English Ceramics Circle*, vol.VII, 1968, pp.59-82

W. D. John, *Nantgarw Porcelain*, Newport, 1948

W. D. John, *Swansea Porcelain*, Newport, 1958

A. E. Jones and L. Joseph, *Swansea Porcelain: Shapes & Decoration*, Cowbridge, 1988

E. Morton Nance, *The Pottery and Porcelain of Swansea and Nantgarw*, London, 1942

7. French Art from Classicism to Post-Impressionism

Vincent Van Gogh Paintings, exh.cat, Rijksmuseum Vincent van Gogh, Amsterdam, 1990

A. Boime, *The Academy and French Painting in the Nineteenth Century*, London, 1971

M. Brunet and M. C. Ross, 'The Sèvres Service of South American Birds at Hillwood', *Art Quarterly*, Autumn 1962, pp.196-208

O. Fairclough, 'Two pieces from the Sèvres Service Iconographique Grec' *National Art-Collections Fund Review*, vol.LXXXVI, 1990, pp.149-52

François-Marius Granet, exh.cat, ed. E. Munhall and J. Focarino, Frick Collection, New York, 1988

R. L. Herbert, *Impressionism*, New Haven and London, 1988

Jean-François-Millet, exh.cat, Arts Council of Great Britain, London, 1976

K. E. Maison, *Honoré Daumier*, London, 1968

The New Painting: Impressionism 1874-1886, exh.cat, Museum of Fine Arts, San Francisco, 1986

Post-Impressionism: Cross-Currents in European Painting, exh.cat, Royal Academy of Arts, London, 1979

Renoir, exh.cat, Arts Council of Great Britain, London, 1985

Rodin Sculpture and Drawings, exh.cat, ed. C. Lampert, Arts Council of Great Britain, London, 1986

P. H. Tucker, *Monet in the '90s*, New Haven and London, 1989

8. Art in Britain from the Foundation of the Royal Academy to the New English Art Club

M. Butlin and E. Joll, *The Paintings of JMW Turner*, New Haven and London, 1984

Constable, exh.cat, ed. L. Parris and I. Fleming-Williams, Tate Gallery, London, 1991

R. Dorment, *Alfred Gilbert*, New Haven and London, 1985

J. Hayes, *The Landscape Paintings of Thomas Gainsborough*, 2 vols, London, 1983

S. C. Hutchinson, *The History of the Royal Academy, 1768-1986*, London, 1986

B. Laughton, *Philip Wilson Steer*, Oxford, 1971

Reynolds, exh.cat, Royal Academy of Arts, London, 1986

The Pre-Raphaelites, exh.cat, Tate Gallery, London, 1984

A. McLaren Young, M. MacDonald, R. Spencer and H. Miles, *The Paintings of James McNeill Whistler*, 2 vols, New Haven and London, 1980

Victorian High Renaissance, exh.cat, Minneapolis Institute of Arts, 1978

9. Wales: Artists, People and Places from the Industrial Revolution to the Depression

D. Bell, *The Artist in Wales*, London, 1957

Collectie Frank Brangwyn, exh.cat, ed. D. Marechal, Stedelijke Musea, Bruges, 1987

Goscombe John at the National Museum of Wales, exh.cat, ed. F. Pearson, National Museum of Wales, Cardiff, 1979

A. P. Ledger, G. L. Pendred and R. A. Hallet, 'The Hafod Service', *Derby International Porcelain Society Newsletter*, vol.XXVII, 1992, pp.5-16

E. Rowan, *Art in Wales: An Illustrated History 1850-1980*, Cardiff, 1985

F. Rutter, *The British Empire Panels*, Benfleet, 1933

The Strange Genius of William Burges 'Art Architect' 1827-1881, exh.cat, National Museum of Wales, Cardiff, 1981

Turner in Wales, exh.cat, ed. A. Wilton, Mostyn Art Gallery, Llandudno, 1984

10. Gwen John and Augustus John

S. Chitty, *Gwen John 1876-1939*, London, 1981

M. Easton and M. Holroyd, *The Art of Augustus John*, London, 1976

M. Holroyd, *Augustus John: A Biography*, 2 vols, London, 1974 and 1975

J. D. Innes at the National Museum of Wales, exh.cat, ed. A. D. Fraser Jenkins, National Museum of Wales, Cardiff, 1975

Gwen John at the National Museum of Wales, exh.cat, ed. A. D. Fraser Jenkins, National Museum of Wales, Cardiff, 1976

A. John, *Autobiography*, London, 1975

C. Langdale, *Gwen John*, New Haven and London, 1987

Portraits by Augustus John: Family, Friends and the Famous, exh.cat, ed. M. L. Evans, National Museum of Wales, Cardiff, 1988

11. From Post-Impressionism to Surrealism

W. Baron, *Sickert*, London, 1973

British Art in the 20th Century: The Modern Movement, exh.cat, Royal Academy of Arts, London, 1987

Cedric Morris, exh.cat, ed. R. Morphet, Tate Gallery, London, 1984

David Jones, exh.cat, ed. P. Hills, Tate Gallery, London, 1981

Eric Gill: Sculpture, exh.cat, ed. J. Collins, Barbican Art Gallery, London, 1992

Exhibition of the National Museum of Wales: Twentieth Century Art in Wales, exh.cat, ed. M. L. Evans, Tokyo Fuji Art Museum, Tokyo, 1989

A. D. Fraser Jenkins, 'Edward Morland Lewis' landscape and photography', *Apollo*, vol.XCIX, 1974, pp.359-60

Magritte, exh.cat, ed. S. Whitfield, Hayward Gallery, London, 1992

Max Ernst, exh.cat, ed. W. Spies, Prestel, Munich, 1991

E. Silber, *The Sculpture of Epstein*, Oxford, 1986

D. Sutton, *André Derain*, London, 1959

12. Art from the Second World War to the Present Day

Ben Nicholson Fifty Years of his Art, exh.cat, Albright-Knox Art Gallery, Buffalo, 1978

The British Neo-Romantics, exh.cat, National Museum of Wales, Cardiff, 1983

Ceri Richards, exh.cat, Tate Gallery, London, 1981

Graham Sutherland, exh.cat, ed. R. Alley, Tate Gallery, London, 1982

Henry Moore, exh.cat, ed. S. Compton, Royal Academy of Arts, London, 1988

John Piper, exh.cat, ed. A. D. Fraser Jenkins, Tate Gallery, London, 1983

Joseph Herman Paintings and Drawings 1940-56, exh.cat, Whitechapel Art Gallery, London, 1956

A Paradise Lost: The Neo-romantic Imagination in Britain 1935-55, exh.cat, ed. D. Mellor, Barbican Art Gallery, London, 1987

The Political Paintings of Merlyn Evans, exh.cat, Tate Gallery, London, 1985

Pop Art, exh.cat, ed. M. Livingstone, Royal Academy of Arts, London, 1991

Reg Butler, exh.cat, Tate Gallery, London, 1983

A School of London: Six Figurative Painters, exh.cat, British Council, London, 1987